Charlie

The Hero by My Side
The true story of a Polar Bear Dog

Helen Thayer…

first woman to ski alone to the Pole.

Adventure Classroom
Snohomish, Washington, USA

Copyright 2021 by Helen Thayer

Published by Adventure Classroom
2230 Connors Road
Snohomish, WA 98290

www.adventureclassroom.org
www.helenthayer.com

All rights reserved. No part of this book may be reproduced in any form without permission in writing from the author.

ISBN: 978-1-7373630-1-9

Book & Cover: 3hats design - Seattle

Acknowledgements

My forever gratitude to Bill who never wavered in his enthusiasm and help in my quest to reach the magnetic North Pole with Charlie.

My thanks to Joe and Tony for Charlie, and to the late Bezal Jesudason and Terry for keeping track of my daily location on my way to the Pole.

And to Roger Greene who flew low over us at our most northerly position. After weeks of total solitude, yours and your passengers' friendly faces as you dipped your aircraft's wings in salute, were a welcome sight.

My thanks to the many Inuit friends whose advise on the ways of the Arctic helped me gain the knowledge I needed to complete the journey to the Pole.

A special thanks to my fellow countryman Sir Edmund Hillary, whose friendship inspired me as a young girl to take the path through life that eventually led me to the magnetic North Pole and a life of adventure.

We owe an enormous debt to John, our *Inuk* friend and wolf biologist, whose help and advice was vital to our success in locating wild wolves and studying them for an entire year. His devotion to these much-maligned animals was a true inspiration.

And to all those renowned scientists who have devoted their lives to the study of these amazing animals and in turn inspired Bill and I to embark on our own journey to live close to and study wild wolves in the true wilderness.

Many thanks to my editor Claire Allen for her advice and friendship.

Dedication

To Charlie, Bill, and my parents.

Charlie

Charlie was a special dog, but didn't know his name...
until one day a special lady, to his village came.
She had a destination, the magnetic North Pole, she must reach.
Charlie knew some secretes, that he alone could teach.

Charlie was a brave dog, as he sniffed the arctic air,
he knew he must protect his friend, from the vicious Polar Bear.
They set off together, just the two of them.
Charlie had a mission, his lady to defend.

In a little Inuit village, Charlie had learned well.
Oh, if he could have talked... the stories he could tell.
His only life was seal meat, the cold, and vast white snow.
Survival was the only thing that Charlie had come to know.

Across the desolate land of ice, the duo made their way.
Charlie stayed beside her, never once to stray.
Seven times throughout their Journey,
the huge, white, stalking, prowlers came.
Seven times, there was Charlie, his cunning presence made.

On the fifth day of their journey,
in the morning arctic air...
out from behind a wall of ice,
stepped a giant polar bear.

Twenty feet before them,
the massive form rose up.
In seconds, he was charging...
would Charlie be enough?

Charlie grabbed the bear's rear leg,
as the bear began to fight.
They went around in circles,
but Charlie held on tight.

Finally, the bear broke lose,
and raced away with Charlie in pursuit.
Charlie's lady waited, afraid of what might be...
Then in cold white distance,
a black spot she could see.

Yes, it was her valiant Charlie,
racing back in graceful strides.
In moments he was back again,
at his lady's side.

It was not an easy journey,
but one they did complete.
Charlie learned a thing called love,
as he stretched at Helen's feet.

Charlie found a new world, one that was serene
Home he went to Washington, oh! It was so green.
Soon he learned a new life, with home and family.
Helen will always be his lady, and he will be her king.
Rhonda Kelly

Introduction

It began in Resolute, one of the world's most remote and cold settled regions, where for several months the sun never rises. It was here that a seemingly ordinary Canadian Inuit sled dog gave birth to a unique pup. As he grew into a muscular adolescent, he proved fearless around bears. His snarling leaps and lightning-quick dodges to avoid a bear's razor-sharp claws and teeth were spectacular, and enough to persuade an attacker to leave for more friendly territory.

At the age of eight, this nameless dog's life changed forever when Helen Thayer, a polar explorer, became his new owner. He was her companion for her historical journey, when she became the first woman to ski alone to the magnetic North Pole. During this journey he risked his own life to save Helen from aggressive, charging polar bears. Descended from both wolves and dogs, Charlie developed into one of the finest polar bear dogs in the world and is known and admired by adventure lovers worldwide.

Later, Charlie was introduced to the dogs, cats and goats on the Thayer family farm and quickly became the ruler of his new animal kingdom. The green grass and trees that he had never seen before was at first investigated with utmost caution. He greeted his first encounter with a genuine Pacific Northwest rain storm with guarded trepidation. The first cat he had ever seen became a best friend.

Continuing his remarkable story, Charlie later became the key that enabled Helen and her husband Bill to live close to wild wolves for a year in the Canadian Arctic when the Thayer's embarked on the monumental quest to observe and understand the ways of wolves in the remote northern wilderness. Charlie's wolf genes provided the pathway to acceptance by three wolf packs, even allowing close interaction with a family's pups.

In a life of well-deserved retirement, he accompanied Helen to her public speaking events and immediately claimed the center of attention and unashamedly basked in his newfound fame. There was no limit to his capacity to win human hearts. This is a true-life adventure story of a once-nameless Inuit dog who exhibited, again and again, his unconditional love and devotion for his human companion—during both challenging adventures and into retirement.

Contents

Acknowledgements & Dedication

Poem to Charlie

Introduction

Chapters

One…	In the Beginning
Two…	I Meet Charlie
Three…	Into the Unknown
Four…	First Encounters
Five…	Bear Attack
Six…	Ice Breakup-Open Water
Seven…	A Showdown for Survival
Eight…	Escaping the Void
Nine…	Far from Anywhere
Ten…	The Storm
Eleven…	Desperate March
Twelve…	The End is in Sight
Thirteen…	Our Triumphant Return
Fourteen…	Home
Fifteen…	Charlie and the Wolves
Sixteen…	Making Friends
Seventeen…	Ravens
Eighteen…	Goodbye
Nineteen…	Ice Wolves
Twenty…	Wolf Camp Two

Epilogue

About the Author

Our story began in Resolute, the small Inuit village of about 250 people on Cornwallis Island in the territory of Nunavut (then called the Northwest Territories). Charlie sits in the snow — lower left.

Charlie - The Hero by My Side

Chapter One — *In the Beginning*

as told by Joe Kallik, an Inuk elder

On a fateful winter's day in November 1980, in the frigid High Arctic of northern Canada, a seemingly ordinary Canadian Inuit sled dog gave birth to a pup who would live for twenty-three years and become a part of polar history, known and admired by adventure lovers around the world. Descended from both wolves and dogs, Charlie was one of the finest polar bear dogs in the world. His story began in Resolute, our small Inuit village of about 250 people on Cornwallis Island in the territory of Nunavut (then called the Northwest Territories). Established in 1947, Resolute is one of the most remote and cold settled regions in the world. Explorers named after the HMS *Resolute*, but in the native language of *Inuktitut* it is called *Qausuittuq* (place with no dawn). From October through January, the sun never rises; winter seizes the sea and land in its icy grasp to shroud the region in three months of darkness.

On this dark day, strong winds raced across the frozen sea ice off the shoreline in yet another of our raging Arctic storms. Chained to the ice on four-foot leads, most of my sled dogs were hunkered down in tight furry balls all in a row, backs to the wind, because dogs are not allowed in buildings in Resolute. One dog, though, had a special mission: she was about to give birth. As the jagged teeth of the sub-zero wind parted her dense black fur, exposing her skin to the needle-like sting of piercing cold, she urgently clawed the cement-hard ice to hollow out a shelter where she could bring her pups into the harsh Arctic world she had known for all of her four years. A shallow depression was the best she could manage, and then she huddled down with her back to the wind. One after the other, four tiny pups arrived, their eyes still closed. Tenderly licking them dry, she snuggled her small family to her furry belly, draping her bushy tail around them to protect them from the wind that could freeze them to death. The pups instinctively pushed their way through their mother's dense fur to her teats to drink their first meal of rich life-giving milk and then, well fed, stayed close to soak up her warmth. In a land of cold, wind, and ice with little shelter, the young mother was the pups' only chance of survival. Amid the roar of the storm, the birth of the pups went unnoticed by the rest of the team of sled dogs. By the next morning the wind had dropped to a stiff chilling northerly breeze, with the temperature hovering around minus 30 degrees Fahrenheit. But saucer-shaped clouds hung in the dark sky, signaling the approach of more strong winds and another storm.

That midmorning when I drove my snow-machine out to feed the dogs, an excited commotion erupted as they watched in anticipation of a meal. I tossed large chunks of frozen seal meat to the dogs, still on their chains. They quickly set to it with ravenous appetites, crunching the bones with teeth prematurely worn by the vigorous work of chewing frozen seal meat for food and then ice for water. Amid the clamor I noticed a large black female dog lying curled on the ice, watching for a piece of meat that might land close by. I walked closer and saw that she was protecting four pups. Knowing that the mother and pups needed shelter from the approaching storm, I untied her chain, scooped up the pups up in one armful, and led the mother to the sheltered side of a twenty-foot-high iceberg imprisoned in the winter sea ice of the frozen bay. Although it would provide only sparse shelter for the new family, they at least would escape the wind.

Tying the mother to a longer chain, I spread a worn brown sack on the ice for her and the pups to lie on, then held out a chunk of seal meat that was more meat than bone. The mother eagerly grabbed it from my hand. Knowing that she needed more food to continue producing milk for her pups, I mounted my snow-machine and raced back to my house in the village. There, with the help of my wife, I placed meat and chunks of fat into a large kettle to thaw over the hot stove. Just like the rest of the dogs in my team, the mother had no name and had known only the life of hard work and vicious storms that these intelligent, hardy dogs often endure. But she was one of my team's strongest and most reliable sled dogs, and I hoped that her pups, whose grandfather had been an Arctic wolf, would grow into valuable members of my team one day.

Returning with the steaming meat, I dumped it in a pile. As the hungry mother gulped down the bounty, I dragged a large wooden packing crate down to the sea ice and left it there beside her for shelter. I wanted her to be able to concentrate on feeding her pups and keeping them warm without having to worry about the wind, which had now developed into a screaming blizzard with temperatures that had already plunged to minus 50 degrees. After finishing the last scrap of meat, the mother gently carried her pups one at a time into the crate.

Three weeks later, with the sun still hiding below the horizon, the pups gradually opened their eyes. Until now they had stayed alongside their mother, buried in her fur, close to her teats. But soon they began to move around within the shelter of the packing crate that was still their home. Over the next few days I kept a close watch and saw the mother attentively feeding and caring for her growing pups while enjoying the extra meat rations I fed her.

    One day that was as dark as the winter night, the mother was chewing her ration of seal meat when a large old-man polar bear silently emerged from the darkness on massive fur-padded paws. Polar bears' sense of smell is crucial to their ability to detect prey, and it is said that they can smell a seal twenty miles away. This bear had picked up the scent of his favorite food and had come to investigate. The dogs immediately reacted to their enemy with snarls and growls as they leaped to the end of their chains to defend against this intruder that they knew could steal their food and perhaps kill them. The wise old bear had been there before, so he knew to keep his distance and watch for his chance to rush in, grab a chunk of meat, and retreat just out of reach of a lunging dog. He paced up and down, barely out of reach of the snarling dogs. Then a slight movement drew his attention to the wooden shelter at one end of the row of dogs. Curious, he approached. The female dog leaped, snarling at the bear, desperate to protect her family. The fearless bear rushed into the crate, mouth agape, reaching out toward the tiny pups. The mother grabbed one furry black bundle and raced into the open away from the lunging bear, not stopping until well clear of the danger. When she looked back, she knew that the bear had killed the rest of her pups. Still clutching the one pup, she raced to hide in the rougher ice, where the six-foot high ridges that had formed in the sea ice a few hundred yards off the coast would provide a hiding place. Having visited the dogs earlier but now halfway back to my house, I heard the uproar behind me. I whipped the snow-machine around and raced back to protect the dogs from the marauder. But I was too late and helplessly watched the mother's desperate flight into the rough ice, carrying one pup in her jaws. The bear lumbered away, leaving a trail of carnage behind him. My heart was broken when I realized that the other pups were gone. This was my favorite dog and I had looked forward to raising her pups, but now there was only one left. The young pup's parents had both been born here. His mother—my favorite—was a Canadian Inuit dog, and his father was a mix of Canadian Inuit dog and Arctic wolf. Occasionally our dogs mate with Arctic wolves and produce young.

    I hurried away and returned with more meat to entice the mother closer so I could clip a chain to her harness and lead her to the safety of the space beneath my house. Unable to resist the tempting meat, the mother allowed me to chain her as she gulped down her reward. Then I cradled the pup under one arm and led the mother to safety. Mother and pup immediately scampered into the dark space beneath the house, where they were protected from both the wind and polar bears.

As the tiny black pup grew, I watched him venture out with his mother to explore the surrounding area. At first, he was clumsy on his short, unsteady legs, but as he explored I saw his confidence growing each day. He played rough-and-tumble games with neighboring pups, but always stayed within sight of his mother.

Then February arrived, and in the clarity of the polar dawn the sun rose briefly above the horizon, signaling a welcome end to winter. Each day its golden disk rose higher in the sky, casting a soft sheen across the still-frozen sea and land. By now the pup, three months old and growing fast, had weaned from his mother's milk and shared the daily meals of meat I provided her. Already he had grown used to wearing a sled-pulling harness.

In mid-May, summer arrived, with twenty-four hours of daylight, higher temperatures, and fewer storms. Now six months old, the young pup, along with other pups of similar age, were well into their training to become sled dogs. But as the pup grew in the summer's warmer temperatures and long days, I noticed that he was larger for his age than the others and even at such an early age had developed a habit of following polar bear tracks at every opportunity. By the time the sun dipped for the last time to signal the beginning of another winter, the pup, now a muscular adolescent and showing promise as an exceptional sled dog, had become fearless around bears, even when a prowling bear attempted to steal food. His snarling leaps and lightning-quick dodges, to avoid those razor-sharp claws and teeth that could rip flesh and kill, were spectacular and quite enough to persuade a bear to leave for more friendly territory.

Increasing darkness and deep cold signaled the start of another long, dark winter. Temperatures dropped below zero, and howling winds again swept the frozen ocean and barren land with icy blasts. Used only occasionally during winter, the dogs remained chained to the sea ice without shelter, as is the custom in these northern parts. In the depths of midwinter, the hamlet became the target of numerous polar bear visits. Instead of chaining the now-year-old dog with the others, I allowed him to roam free to chase away any approaching bear. It worked. The dog raced after the bears, chasing them out of the village and far out onto the sea ice. Over the long winter he developed his bear-chasing skills and kept their raids to a minimum. As soon as the long darkness of winter gave way to day-lit spring days, again I hitched the dogs to a sled to prepare for the summer's seal and polar bear hunts. As the young dog grew stronger, his stamina increased and he kept pace with the team for increasingly longer distances until he easily ran all the way with them, even when they traveled many miles from the hamlet, far out across the sea ice. He was now a full member of the sled team, but I saw that his favorite pastime was chasing polar bears, and especially the polar bear hunts. I became increasingly impressed by his skill and fearlessness around these bears. By the end of the summer the youngster had grown muscular, with the long-distance stamina of a powerful Inuit dog. Now that he was an adult his days of play were over. It was time to learn the discipline of a working sled dog. But most important to me and to the hamlet's residents, he had become a dependable deterrent when polar bears approached.

As time went on, the black dog became my favorite. He was a regular on my team, especially during polar bear hunts. Then one day, as the team dashed across the sea ice far out beyond the shore, the sled hit rough ice and suddenly overturned. My leg was crushed beneath the heavy sled. My hunting companions took me back to the hamlet. After a long recovery it was obvious that my hunting days were over. Age and injury had slowed my body. It was time to pass my dogs on to another who could properly care for them. I gave them away to various family members and friends, but the black dog, my favorite, I gave to my friend Tony. He was a particularly caring dog owner and first-rate hunter.

Then, a short time later, at the age of eight, this special dog's life changed forever when a polar explorer named Helen Thayer became his new owner. He entered polar history when he walked at her side to protect her from polar bears as she became the first woman to travel alone to the magnetic North Pole.

As I write this, I think back to that tragic day when the pup lost his siblings, and his mother, fearless and determined, was racing to save his life. The pup inherited his mother's traits of intelligence and determination. To know that he has gained a place in polar history makes me proud to have been his original owner.

Charlie - The Hero by My Side

I meet Charlie

Chapter Two — *I Meet Charlie*

My name is Helen Thayer, and at fifty years old, I embarked on an expedition to the magnetic North Pole to become the first woman to travel alone on foot to any of the world's poles without the aid of a dog team, snowmobile, aircraft, or outside support. I was motivated by the fact that this expedition would not only realize my personal goal of traveling alone to the Pole, but would also be shared with others via an educational organization I developed, named Adventure Classroom. I didn't know yet that it would also be shared with a remarkable and heroic dog named Charlie.

I had already enjoyed many years in sports, when I represented three countries in international track and field: New Zealand, the country of my birth; Guatemala, where my husband flew a helicopter, and the United States. Later, after I won the United States national luge championship, I became a member of the national team. But my first love was mountain climbing and the extreme challenges that high-altitude mountains presented. Sir Edmund Hillary, the first person to summit Mount Everest and a close family friend, had been my climbing hero since I began climbing mountains with my parents at nine years old. I continued my climbing career and as I became more experienced, I climbed many high mountains worldwide. In 1986, when I stood on the 24,590-foot summit of Tajikistan's Peak Communism and took in the spectacular 360-degree view into China on one side and Afghanistan on the other, I wondered how I could share my experiences with schoolchildren who might never have this opportunity. Would it be possible to use my expedition experiences in a career of creating educational programs?

After summiting that peak, we descended to base camp and after packing our gear we drove to the city of Osh in Kyrgyzstan to catch our flight to Moscow and on to Seattle. During the long flight home, I mused over my new goal. First, I decided on the name Adventure Classroom. But where should I begin? After considering various destinations, it occurred to me that the compass that had faithfully guided me to safety on many expeditions always pointed to the magnetic North Pole. The magnetic Pole is crucial to navigators at sea, in the air, and on land. And it was a place that I knew would be a stark contrast to the mountains I'd just spent so much time conquering.

Could I ski alone to the place my compass needle pointed to? I remembered reading about polar bears. My fascination with these animals, who live a life of survival in one of the coldest climates on earth, confirmed my decision that this would be the perfect expedition to launch Adventure Classroom. I was eager to discuss my plans with Bill, my husband, best friend, and a commercial helicopter pilot. I knew that his own outdoor experiences would give him a good understanding of the journey I envisioned.

He was immediately enthusiastic. "A woman has never skied alone to any of the world's poles. It's a great idea." Together we charted out an environmentally low-impact journey—traveling alone, on foot, without a dog team or snowmobile—on which I would pull a sled for 364 miles across an ice-covered ocean, with only the food and equipment I could carry. When loaded, the sled would weigh 160 pounds.

I knew little about the magnetic North Pole, so I spoke to The Geological Survey of Canada scientists in Ottawa who track the magnetic Pole's yearly location. I learned that within the vicinity of the Pole, a magnetic compass is actually useless, its needle turning lazily and unpredictably in all directions due to the lack of horizontal magnetic pull. In 1988, the year I made the journey, the magnetic North Pole was located almost eight hundred miles above the Arctic Circle, south of King Christian Island, which is a barren, ice-covered island swept by sub-zero Arctic winds. This lonely, uninhabited island, situated at the northern boundary of the magnetic Pole's region, was to be my most northerly destination. Helena Island, situated within the southern boundary of the Pole's region, would be my most southerly destination. To provide a comprehensive educational program for Adventure Classroom I decided to ski a complete circumnavigation of the entire Pole area. I was warned of many dangers. Ridges of teeter-tottering blocks of ice and wide water leads—places where storms had split the ice apart—could necessitate long detours to cross without falling into the ocean. A dip into the frigid waters would give me no chance to get out before freezing to death. These daunting hazards were far outweighed by the greatest danger of all: polar bears. They live on the sea ice, hunting seals along my intended route. Some of the most intelligent hunters in the animal world, they sometimes hunt humans for food when presented with the opportunity. To gain a better understanding of the challenges, I traveled to the northern Canadian village of Resolute to gain firsthand experience skiing across the frozen ocean and camping in a place inhabited by polar bears. In keeping with their kind and generous culture, several Inuit residents took me out onto the sea ice and showed me the tactics I should use when faced by a bear. These masters of Arctic survival taught me to read bear tracks, analyze Arctic weather signs, and interpret various sea ice conditions. But first they urged me to abandon my plan to travel on foot.

"The men don't hunt that far north. Too much wind and cold and too far," they told me. An *Inuk* elder named Willy was adamant in his attempt to persuade me that I should travel by snowmobile or a dog team. "Either way you'll be safer. Polar bears won't bother you. The noise of the snowmobile will keep them away and you'll have the speed to escape. Or you could use a team: polar bears normally don't approach a traveling dog team, and at night you'll have many voices to warn you. But if you're on foot and all by yourself, the bears will see you as an easy target. They might kill you." Their advice was well meaning, but eventually they accepted the fact that I was determined to ski alone without the support of a dog team or snowmobile.

In March 1988, after two years of preparation and testing equipment, I was ready to embark on the new adventure. I flew north from Seattle and established my base camp at Resolute. Nearby was the last human habitat, the Polaris Mine. Many past expeditions had used the mine as their starting place, therefore making it the most logical point to begin my solo expedition. My base camp was the High Arctic International Explorers Inn, the traditional base for polar expeditions. Run by Bezal and Terry Jesudason, the inn was equipped with sophisticated radio equipment that would enable them to listen for my nightly radio calls to establish my daily position and provide me with weather forecasts. My exact location would always be known in case of emergency. I was eager to get started, but I didn't know that the most vital part of my preparation was yet to come.

One day in Resolute, as I was preparing my sled to go out on the ice for another training run, an *Inuk* villager named Tony who had just returned from a hunting trip sought me out in the equipment shed. Concerned about my safety, he tried to persuade me to at least take three or four dogs to pull my supplies and act as a polar bear deterrent.

"No, I don't want to travel by dog team," I said, "but I've wondered about taking one dog to walk at my side to warn me of any bears and to be on guard at night."

"I can help you," he said, "I've a dog you can take. He's trained to warn the hamlet of polar bears when they come in off the ice, and he knows how to take care of himself." Soon Tony returned with a big black husky. I immediately fell in love with him. He didn't look particularly brave or ferocious, though, and as I patted him, I wondered what he would do if confronted by a bear. I couldn't quite imagine this docile animal chasing a bear out of the village, and wondered if Tony had been exaggerating just a bit. But having been around dogs all my life, and being an avid dog lover, I sensed that there was something about this nameless dog that I could trust. When I led the dog away, he followed willingly and seemed happy at my side. At this point I had absolutely no knowledge of this dog's background. The Inuit don't treat their dogs as pets. The dogs have no names and lead a harsh life. It wasn't until we returned from the expedition that I learned of his history from Joe, an *Inuk* elder. For now, he was just a nameless Inuit dog—that I had spent my last one hundred dollars on in hopes that he might be useful around polar bears. Now to name him! As I looked into the dog's soft eyes, I thought of the name Charlie. It seemed to fit him, so he became Charlie and my new teammate. Offering him the first human kindness he had ever experienced, I hugged him close. Dogs were not allowed into the buildings in Resolute, but I was determined that he would not spend time unsheltered out on the ice. After a great deal of searching, I eventually found a sad relic of a boat that had long ago been stripped of paint and now lay abandoned on its side, trapped in the shore ice. I tied Charlie's lead to an upright, and after eating his dinner he disappeared inside the tattered remnants of the boat's cabin to sleep. It was plain that he appreciated the shelter. As crude and basic as it might be, it was far better than anything he had ever experienced, and he lost no time in taking full advantage of these brand-new sleeping arrangements.

The next morning, I could hardly wait for the first rays of daylight to wash over the horizon so that I could take breakfast to my new friend. Rather than feed him his usual meal of frozen seal meat, I fed him dry dog food that had been given to me. Although unused to such food, Charlie gobbled it up and looked for more, but I rationed it carefully to give him time to become accustomed to it. Terry, from the inn, gave me an old aluminum pan to use for Charlie's food bowl. I was also given a new red padded harness and a small lightweight child's plastic sled for Charlie to haul. With Charlie suitably equipped and looking splendid in his new harness, we were ready to establish ourselves as a team. I loaded Charlie's food, along with assorted items such as a spare lead and collar, onto my sled and left him with about fifteen pounds to pull. My reasoning was that if he was to watch for bears and protect me if needed, I would rather he not be tired out by pulling a heavier sled. And I knew that although his food greatly increased my load, the weight would be reduced by two pounds each day. Tony had advised me to keep Charlie tethered so that he would always be at my side instead of following bear tracks to find the tracks' owner, risking injury or even death. After outfitting him with a blue nylon collar and a sturdy dog lead with a quick-release clip, I attached his lead to a loop on my sled harness at my waist, making it impossible for him to go anywhere without me.

The next three days were spent training: getting Charlie used to the routine of walking at my side while becoming accustomed to my skis. The first hour was a puzzle to him. At first, he stared down at my skis as he walked, apparently wondering, *What in the world is she walking on?* After a few yards he stopped and tested them with a touch of his nose, and jumped back as if startled by their feel. Then, apparently having decided something was not right about those odd-looking long sticks, he proceeded to walk at the far end of his lead, as far away from the skis as possible. I urged him closer, but to no avail, and decided that he would have to take his own time to get used to walking alongside my skis. We had traveled three miles out across the ice before he accepted the fact that the skis were harmless and he could safely walk closer to my side. The entire performance did nothing to instill my confidence in his ability to chase a polar bear. *If my skis scare him,* I thought, *what in the world will an 800-pound bear mean to him?* By now I believed that Tony had been sadly mistaken regarding this dog's polar bear-chasing abilities. *Well,* I thought, *any dog is probably better than no dog at all.* Then, an hour or so later, in a new and entirely unexpected development, he appeared to decide that the skis could serve to increase his personal comfort. He stood squarely on both skis, apparently to avoid walking on the cold, hard ice. *After all,* he might have thought, *if she can use these things to walk on, why shouldn't I do the same?* This business of adjusting to me traveling on skis had now reached ridiculous proportions. I explained to him that standing on my skis anchored me to the spot, so travel was impossible, then gave him a gentle shove. After some hesitation he reluctantly stepped back onto the ice. The entire situation struck me as vastly amusing. It would be an understatement to say that I was by now skeptical of not only his polar bear protection abilities, but also his ability to even withstand the rigors of the journey that lay ahead of us. I could imagine him taking cover *behind* me if we met a bear. So far, his only concern seemed to be to figure out what I was doing and how he could increase his own comfort. He was obviously highly intelligent. He quickly responded to his name and displayed an incredible ability to figure out ways not only to adjust to his new situation, but also to increase his personal well-being. With some resignation I decided that if nothing else, he would make a good companion. He'd be more of a pet than a protector. At day's end he looked on with studied interest as I erected my tent. Then, after circling the tent and sniffing the nylon walls, he suddenly raised a leg to send a stream coursing down the tent wall. This was not my idea of good manners. Next, he wandered over to the tent doorway to take a brief look inside, but apparently decided he was better off outside. He lay down alongside my sled to watch further developments. It was time for dinner, and due to the performance over my skis

I was concerned that he might panic when I lit the stove; when lit, it sounded like a miniature blowtorch. I need not have worried. He watched with only mild interest, as if the entire process of camping held no real interest to him. But his attitude changed dramatically when I produced a meal of human food: rice, freeze-dried vegetables, and mashed potatoes. I placed half in his pan. After he took one inquisitive sniff, the whole lot disappeared in a flash. Then, with an air of expectancy, he looked hard at my bowl. It was the first human food he had ever tasted. I was hungry, but decided that in the interest of bonding together, he could eat mine and I would cook another meal. That did the trick. From then on, we were not only a team but also best buddies. The next day I wisely visited the local store to buy a few more human food supplies. It was obvious that Charlie would insist that I share.

Because my confidence in Charlie as my first line of defense against the bears was tentative at best, I also carried a .338 Winchester Magnum rifle and a flare gun. Not being a hunter, I didn't want to have to shoot a bear. I planned to fire flares to land in front of a bear, in the hopes that the flare's red flame and acrid curtain of smoke would discourage an attack. Later, when asked how many flares I carried, my answer was, "Enough to do an army proud." I was determined to be prepared.

The first time I put on Charlie's harness and hitched his sled to it, he peered up at me in consternation, as if to ask, *What am I supposed to do now?* When I urged him forward, his whole attitude radiated outrage. The only sled he had ever seen or pulled was the large Inuit *komatik* sled used to haul heavy loads, and then always as a member of a dog team. His answer to my order to move ahead and pull this tiny sled was to promptly sit down in protest. He was not going to pull that thing he was hitched to. I tried to gently urge him forward in a tone that I hoped would instill confidence in this new situation. But he merely sat on his haunches and even turned his face away, as if he didn't hear me. When my voice rose in indignation, he turned toward me with an interrogative look that seemed to say with insufferable mildness, *Oh, did you speak?* Momentarily beyond speech, I stood there and stared at the performance unfolding before me. Then, with notable restraint, I hooked his harness to a lead and gently pulled him forward. With a hard glint of suspicion in his eye and very little grace, he at last consented to obediently walk at my side with the sled following. *At least*, I thought, *we're beginning to make progress.* From the beginning I had realized that Charlie had a strong-willed alpha nature, but I thought he had already bonded with me and accepted me as his alpha. On being asked to pull this object that he apparently considered to be beneath his dignity, though, he seemed to feel it was time to express his indignation and make known his boundaries. But by day's end he seemed to accept that pulling the sled was to become a permanent arrangement, so he might as well do as I asked, although it obviously pained him to do so.

At midday on the third day of training, after we had spent an uneventful morning out on the ice, I decided to change course before returning to camp and investigate an area of low ridges of ice to the west. Just as we entered the first ten-to-fifteen-foot-high pinnacles, Charlie unexpectedly stopped and growled. He stared ahead into the maze of ridges that rose in our path. I squinted to see through the dazzling glare, but at first saw nothing. Charlie's growls grew louder. He pulled hard at the end of his lead, wanting to go after something out there. Then I glimpsed a large bear just as he disappeared behind a low ridge of ice. I grabbed my flare gun and rifle and turned to take a path back through the ridges toward camp, keeping a wary eye open in case the bear circled around toward us. Sure enough, just as we were clearing the last ridge Charlie, with a deafening growl, leaped to the end of his lead, facing the bear, which now stood only twenty feet away, watching us. Snarling and growling, Charlie strained on his lead to reach the bear. After a few brief moments the bear, apparently impressed by Charlie's aggressive snarls and leaps, turned and loped away to disappear amid the rough ice ahead. I watched Charlie in astonishment. In an instant he had changed from a docile, lovable companion to a growling, fierce bundle of pent-up ferocious energy, intent on chasing a polar bear. I was ecstatic. Now I saw what Tony had meant. Charlie was indeed a polar bear dog! My confidence in his ability to warn me of any bears rose dramatically, and I knew that we were ready to start our journey to the Pole.

Hooking up.

We were ready to start our journey to the Pole.

Our starting point was the Polaris Mine

Chapter Three — *Into The Unknown*

On March 29, Charlie and I were flown in a DC-3 aircraft about fifty-seven miles to our start point at the Polaris Mine. We were the only passengers on the plane, which was filled with a cargo of food that included large sacks of potatoes to resupply the mine staff. Not knowing how Charlie would react to flying, I kept a tight grip on his collar as we took off from the ice runway. His first reaction was one of surprise, and he immediately climbed onto my lap. Ninety-four pounds of dog in my lap was not going to work for either of us. With considerable effort I pushed and shoved him onto the window-side half of my seat while I sat wedged between him and a large sack of potatoes. It wasn't a dignified way to begin our journey, but it would have to do. He quickly relaxed and leaned heavily on me while appearing to enjoy the flight. I was not quite so happy. The potatoes were pressing into my ribs, the seat was cold and hard, and I was peering ahead through Charlie's thick, black fur coat. By halfway through the flight, Charlie was leaning on me to such an extent that I sat more on the potatoes than the seat. Once more, Charlie in his intelligent way had figured out a suitable tactic that would ensure his personal comfort.

Our flight took us across a barren, frozen landscape that looked ominously uninviting, but I reasoned that once we had escaped from this cold, remarkably cramped, potato-filled airplane, my confidence in the journey ahead would return. We landed on another frozen runway and Charlie and I stepped from the plane into a bitterly cold wind. The mine supervisor met us and led us to our overnight accommodations. Charlie's consisted of the equipment shed, while I was escorted to comfortable mine living quarters.

We were treated like royalty. An admiring crowd gathered around Charlie, which he took in stride, tail fanning back and forth, pleased at his reception. His friendly demeanor impressed everyone, leading some to tell me that they had expected a fierce, dominant polar bear dog. "We expected an attack dog," was one comment, "but he seems more like a big lovable pet that I would take home to my kids."

Next morning after breakfast at the cafeteria, I called Terry at base camp and told her that we were about to leave, and that I would relay my location each night. I went to join Charlie. Overnight he had been showered with kindness. When Tim Sewell, working the overnight shift on equipment, had walked into the dark shed and turned on the light, he told me, "I just about dropped dead from fright when a large black dog confronted me." He recovered enough to call on the intercom to report what he had discovered—and was told who the dog was and why he was there. Tim, a dog lover, told me, "I patted him and he looked so lonely I decided to feed him something special. I rounded up some of my buddies and we went to the kitchen, got us a bucket of meat, and took it to Charlie. He ate it in record time. Then we gathered up all the old coveralls we could find and made a soft bed for him. You sure have a great dog there. Take care of him." Charlie greeted me as he would an old friend and eagerly followed me outside. I had missed him overnight and was relieved and happy to be reunited with him.

Then I located my sled in a side shed. I stared at it in disbelief. Gloves were sticking out of a food bag, a spare hat sat draped over the stove, Charlie's food pan hung to one side barely attached to the sled, and my sleeping bag had been tucked beneath a pile of fuel bottles. Various other items were scattered about in odd places. Evidently a heavy box had fallen onto the sled during our flight to the mine and the impact had loosened the main tie-down rope, sending things flying. After unloading the sled from the plane, the damage had been discovered and they had loaded it all back on the sled. There was nothing to do but start over and reload the mess into something that resembled a decently packed sled. Charlie didn't display much interest in my reloading project until I reached for the food bags. He pressed forward to inspect the contents. "No, Charlie, stay back," I told him. At first, deaf to my request, he ignored me and pushed further into a bag, intent on inspecting its contents. I grabbed his collar and again said *"No!"* but with greater emphasis. With reluctant resignation he finally agreed to step back, but not too far, just in case another opportunity presented itself. I began sorting through the muddled chaos, but decided that I would repack when I set up camp at day's end.

With temperatures hovering around minus 40 degrees, I pulled my sled down to where the shore ice met the sea ice. Charlie walked close at my side, harnessed to his sled, attached with a lead to my sled-hauling waist belt. The date was March 30, 1988, and Charlie and I were about to start the most challenging journey of our lives. It was nine A.M. and time to get going. After some last-minute photos and goodbyes, we stepped out onto the sea ice. The first quarter mile was a rough jumble of icy pinnacles, some as high as ten feet, broken and leaning at odd angles, tortured by the constant rising and falling of tides that groan and sigh under the great weight they lift. Frustrated, I gave up trying to ski through the narrow gaps that jammed my sled. Laying my skis on top of the sled, I pulled and tugged it through the gaps by hand, then helped Charlie through with his sled. In my imagination before leaving, I saw myself skiing off into the mysterious distance to conquer who-knows-what. Instead, here I was, without skis, hauling my sled through by hand. Definitely not the impressive start I had envisioned. Fortunately, a quick look back to shore told me that my send-off group had left to resume their various jobs and weren't there to see our less-than-spectacular start. Charlie patiently waited until I pulled his sled through. It must have seemed strange to him to watch me. He was more used to a life as a member of a dog team charging headlong through the shore ice without so much as a pause while pulling an Inuit *komatik*. Finally, after a few more pulls, we were through. Beyond, I was greeted by the glorious sight of smooth ice, streaked with ridges up to six inches high called sastrugi, separated by patches of hard-packed snow. I donned my skis and sled harness, and after checking Charlie's harness we set off. At last our journey had really begun. Setting a northerly course, I shut the door on civilization. We would see no other people for almost a month. We would be entirely alone in an environment that does not welcome humans.

Now free of the unstable shore ice, my attention returned to bears. Charlie strode easily at my side, his thick black coat shining in the sunshine. This was his home. Polar bears, freezing temperatures, and ice were not new to him. I wondered what he would think if he knew that his companion was terrified of meeting just one bear. He raised his nose to test the air for the scent of bears and seals, both scents familiar to him all his life. I took courage from having him at my side, and decided that I would have to trust him to warn me of any bears, hopefully even before I saw them. Suddenly, the roar of an approaching snowmobile broke the silence. It was Don, a mine employee, coming to warn me that he had found bear tracks close by. "It looks as though a bear might be hidden in the rough stuff somewhere ahead of you." Then, wishing Charlie and me a safe journey, he roared away in the direction of the mine, leaving us alone in the silent, windswept void that surrounded us. Realizing that I might be playing hide-and-seek with a bear, I instinctively pulled Charlie closer. Already he was a comfort. My courage was not bolstered by the thought that to a bear I would be food and nothing else.

A ten-mile-per-hour wind drifted in from the north. At minus 32 degrees the wind stung my face, forcing me to stop and put on my dark-blue neoprene face mask to protect my face from freezing. The cloudless blue sky, made pale by the reflecting ice, stretched for miles across Bathurst Island to the west, its dark shape a contrast to the brilliant white ice that crowded its shores. Skiing kept me reasonably warm, but the penetrating cold made it impossible to stop any longer than ten minutes to eat a quick snack. The cold of the gradually increasing headwind seeped through the lighter insulated jacket I usually wore when traveling. At my second stop I grabbed my big down parka and put it on. Although its insulation made me look like the Michelin tire man, it provided welcome warmth. Charlie offered no comment on my fashion. His thick, black fur coat was all he needed.

Each time I stopped and took out the day's snack bag, Charlie pressed forward in eager anticipation of accepting his share. The menu consisted of a warm high-carbohydrate drink from my thermos, followed by a handful of high-fat butter crackers and chocolate peanut butter cups. At each stop I gave Charlie a handful of his dry dog food. But his menu preference proved to be my food. At the first stop I told him as I handed him his dog food, "No, Charlie, my food isn't for you." My explanation held no interest for him. His mind was set on my food and that was that! As I ate, I turned my back on him to avoid his begging look, but that wasn't a deterrent; he walked around to once more face me. I felt my willpower weakening. Knowing that we had many days ahead of us, I sensed that Charlie would find a way to make me share. And, of course, he did!

For the first four hours of travel, we crossed the fresh tracks of a female bear and her two cubs several times. They appeared to be traveling north ahead of us, but so far, in spite of keeping a sharp eye out, I hadn't seen them. An excited Charlie pressed his nose to the tracks, eager to follow them. I wasn't happy with our progress. We still had over 360 miles to go. Frequent stops to scan for bears had seriously slowed our progress. I had to find a way to watch for bears and at the same time increase our speed.

Now and then we crossed bear paw prints that were as much as twelve inches across. Judging by their size, these were males. In eager anticipation of an exciting chase, Charlie pulled on his lead to follow. It was only after I tugged back on his lead and told him, "No, Charlie, we're not going there," that we were able to continue on our way north. As the day progressed, I sensed that Charlie had tuned into my fear of bears. By noon, every time we crossed bear tracks, he no longer tried to follow, and instead pressed in closer to my leg, to the point that I sometimes had to stop to regain my balance when his weight was too much. It was as if he was trying to tell me that he would make it all okay. The comfort of not only having him at my side but feeling his warm body pressed against my leg helped calm my nerves as I skied ahead into the white glare that pressed in from all sides and merged with the vague outlines of distant islands.

Although this was our first day, Charlie already seemed comfortable walking at my side, but I also recognized his trust in me. This trust would be new to him because up to now he had never had a reason to expect human kindness. Even the little blue sled that followed at his heels seemed no longer objectionable to him.

Often the bear tracks were crisscrossed with the tiny paw prints of Arctic foxes. These foxes with long bushy tails and coats of dense white fur follow polar bears, hoping to scavenge leftovers from seal kills. On land they eat tiny rodents called lemmings.

My map, which I kept in the upper left-hand pocket of my jacket, was one of my most important navigational tools. The afternoon wore on as the sun swung south and then west. After traveling eleven miles, I stopped to camp a quarter-mile offshore. As the sun slowly disappeared over the horizon, taking with it its meager warmth, a deep penetrating chill descended over us like a heavy, cold blanket. The temperature plunged thirteen degrees over the next hour to minus 45 degrees. A hazy band of pale purple swept the horizon. The wind, which had gradually increased throughout the day, was a steady twenty-five miles per hour by nightfall. The ice, in contrast to its daytime dazzling glare, was bathed in a gloomy, cold, gray light. In the heavy silence of the approaching darkness, nothing moved. Now that I had stopped and the sun had disappeared, the cold was unrelenting. I hurried to set up camp. My first task was to take a hollow titanium six-inch long ice screw from my equipment bag and twist it firmly into the ice to provide an anchor to attach Charlie's lead. After hunting for Charlie's food pan on his sled, I finally found it on my own. I fed him an ample helping of his food, which he began gulping down even before my hand left the pan. Concerned that Charlie was sleeping on the cold hard ice, I slid a spare jacket beneath him, but he simply rose and, with a deep sigh, moved over and curled up to sleep on the bare ice. An ice bed was all that he had ever known, and in his independent spirit he was going to do it his way. It was the first of many lessons he would teach me on this journey.

My sled load was still a disastrous mess. Nothing was where I usually kept it, and the time spent searching for gear made my hands ache with deep cold. I was wearing a thin pair of liner gloves under a medium-weight pair to give my hands better dexterity as I traveled, but now I was racing to find my insulated mitts before frostbite set in. They should have been in the front of my sled under my down jacket, but they weren't. I had no time for an organized search, so I dumped everything out onto the ice and the mitts tumbled out. By now my fingers were white and felt like blocks of wood. I plunged my hands into the mitts' warm depths and windmilled my arms in a desperate attempt to pump blood into my hands and fingers, hoping to keep frostbite away. Ten minutes later, I felt the first effects of my efforts as the searing-hot pain of returning circulation began. At least the agony of my fingers told me they were still alive and not frozen beyond recovery. To continue the warming process, I ran in tight circles, still swinging my arms. I didn't dare look at Charlie. Surely, he must have been puzzled as he observed my frantic activity. Eventually my hands were acceptably warm and the hot agony in my fingers was bearable, although it turned out they had not escaped frostbite. With painful, barely functional hands I erected my blue nylon tent and anchored it to the ice with six ice screws. After I had unloaded my sled and placed my down sleeping bag, stove, and clothing in the tent, I laid the nylon bag containing thermometers, wind gauge, data log book, journal, and pencils on my sleeping bag, ready to enter the day's events.

Next, I turned my attention to preparing a warm meal and drink. First, I had to light my stove and would be unable to hear anything over its roar. I needed Charlie to bear-watch while I cooked, but he was already curled up on the ice, asleep. I called his name but received no response. I gently prodded him awake. His only reaction was to open a sleepy eye, then, apparently having decided that whatever I wanted would just have to wait, he promptly tucked his nose under his bushy tail and resumed his sleep. I realized that I would have to learn to trust his judgment concerning bears. His extremely keen sense of smell would detect a bear even before he saw it. To turn my back on a sleeping Charlie and light that noisy stove was a test of sheer trust. But when I tried to push the tube that led from the fuel bottle into a slot in the stove, the pain in my fingers was overwhelming, so I gave up and ate a cold meal of odds and ends and the last of my warm drink from my thermos. It was not what I had envisioned as my first meal of the expedition, but it would have to do until I could figure out a way to work with my painful fingers. Halfway through my meal, Charlie, apparently sensing that food was again on the schedule, appeared in the tent doorway, ready to share. His intense stare at my bowl clearly demanded that I give him at least a portion of my meal. I passed him some crackers. They instantly disappeared, and with a satisfied grunt he lay down just outside the doorway while he kept an eye on me in case more food would be forthcoming.

It was almost eight o'clock, the scheduled time for my first radio call to base camp. Anchoring my radio antenna to the ice with a sharp stake, I ran the antenna through the binding of one ski that was standing on end next to my tent. I shoved the batteries into the radio then pressed the transmitter button and called, "Kiwi expedition calling eight-one-five Resolute. Over!" Terry's cheerful voice answered. After I gave her my location, she relayed a weather report and asked, "Did you see any bears?" When I said, "No," she sounded relieved: "Good, I hope you don't meet any."

Next, I faced the task of repacking my sled. Although the pain in my fingers ranged from agonizing to just painful, they were still usable. At last, after a lot of rearranging, my sled looked a perfect picture of neatness and organization. I anchored Charlie's and my sleds just outside the tent with an ice screw. My skis were outside the tent door within easy reach. My snow shovel, rifle, and flare gun were in the tent vestibule in case of need.

After writing the day's events and my location in my journal with fingers that protested even the simple task of holding a pencil, my thoughts turned to slipping into my sleeping bag to escape the raw cold. I checked on Charlie, who was already fast asleep. Watching him sleep on ice bothered my conscience. He had refused the jacket I had pushed under him earlier, but I wondered if a spare gunnysack that had come with his dog food might be more to his liking. I tried to push it under him, but the reproachful look he gave me convinced me to stop fussing and let him sleep.

After one last look around for bears, with throbbing hands and gritted teeth, I painfully eased off my boots and climbed into my sleeping bag, thankful that the first day was over. I lay looking at the tent walls and ceiling, wondering how long would it take for a bear to rip through the thin nylon. Of course, I knew that the answer was no time at all—definitely not a comforting thought. But I reasoned that there was no point in lying awake and worrying about bears. In spite of frostbitten hands that now showed nine bloody, blistered fingers, I was in excellent physical condition and the day's skiing hadn't tired me at all. Charlie slept just outside the door, and I would have to have faith he would warn me of any approaching bear. I called out, "Goodnight, Charlie." There was no response, so I too fell asleep.

I set out with Charlie at my side

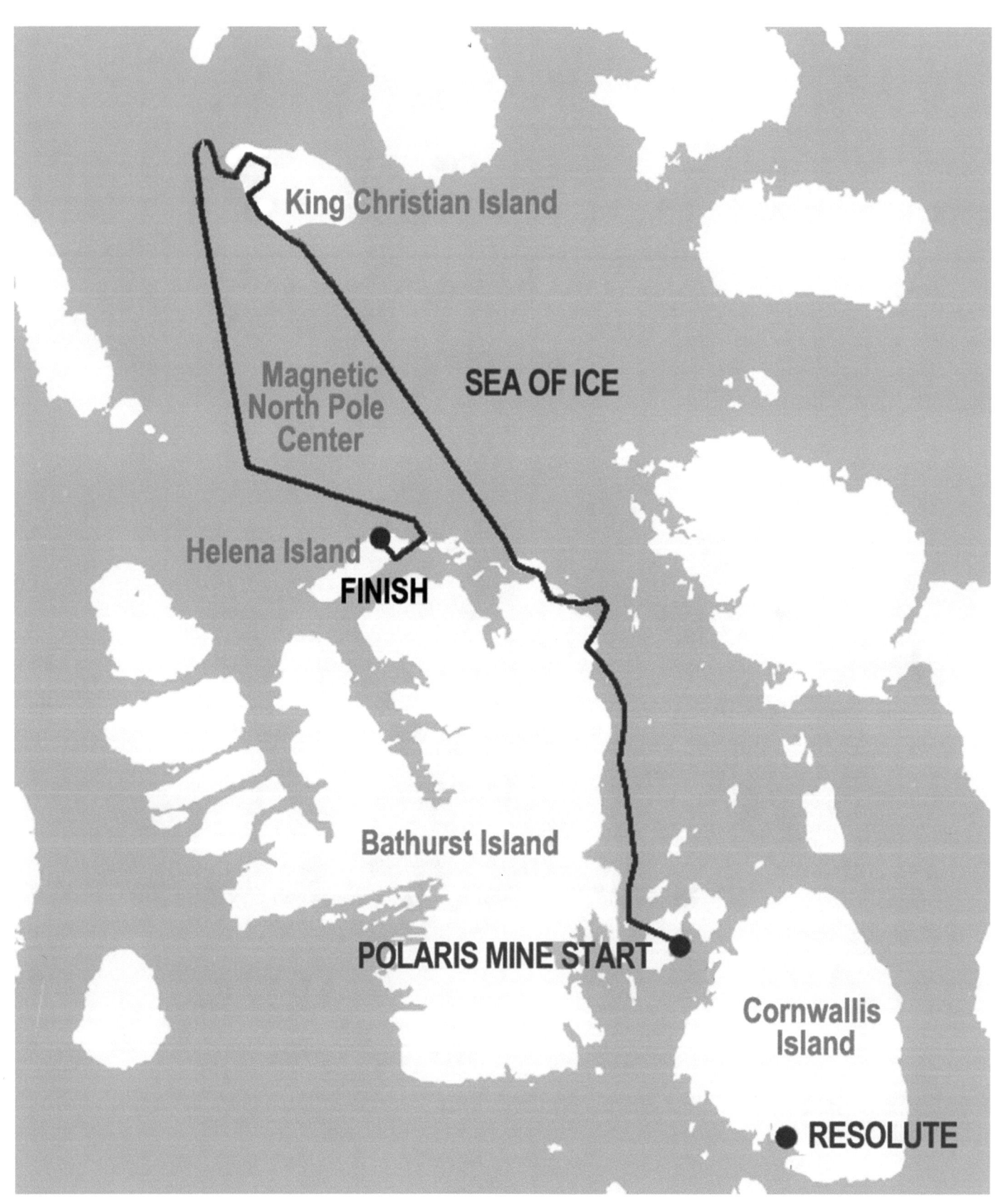

The route–mostly across Arctic sea ice–passes through the Pole's central position and circumnavigates the entire Magnetic North Pole region.

Bear paw print in the snow

Breaking camp to start the second day

Chapter Four — *First Encounters*

After a restless night's sleep I was up at 5:30 A.M. to greet Charlie, who was already up and waiting expectantly beside his food pan. Overnight, the large blood blisters on my fingers had grown to reach all the way down to the second joint of each finger, except for my left little finger, which had somehow escaped freezing. To prevent the blisters from breaking and turning my hands into a bloody raw mess, I left my liner gloves on as protection. The minus 41 degrees on my thermometer, together with my throbbing hands, made the morning most unappealing. The urge to return to my sleeping bag was hard to resist, but the only way to cover the miles ahead was to start the day.

When I hugged Charlie good morning, he greeted me with a swipe of his soft tongue across my face. I poured dog food into his pan, then set to work to melt ice for the day's water for us both. While I ate my breakfast of granola, milk powder, coconut flakes and butter, Charlie stood by watching in anticipation of receiving his share of my food. Much to his frustration I ignored him. Judging by his begging, short sharp yips, and even whines, he felt I was grossly uncaring about his well-being. Ignoring him wasn't working. I handed him a few crackers. He grabbed them and lay down to enjoy his snack. Again, victory was his! With breakfast over, it was time to pull down the tent and finish packing.

As I was figuring out a way to twist the ice screws out of the ice with hands that were screaming in protest, Charlie suddenly emitted a long growl from the depths of his throat. Dropping the ice screws, I spun to follow his gaze. A female bear and her two cubs had discovered us. Still two hundred yards away, she marched forward without pausing. She stopped only a hundred feet away. With a pounding heart, I grabbed the rifle. Charlie, his lead still attached to an anchor, leaped forward, snarling with bared teeth. I fired a warning rifle shot to her left, but the deafening sound of the .338 Winchester had no effect. She no doubt was used to the rifle-like sounds of the moving ice pack. Without breaking stride, she marched closer and closer. Grabbing the flare gun, I fired a flare that landed a little to her right, but still she didn't stop. With nerves as tight as violin strings, I fired another to land in front of her, almost at her feet. She paused a moment, then fixed her gaze on Charlie, who exploded forward with a deafening snarl, ferocious and frothing at the mouth.

The mother, now only fifty feet away, was taken aback by the tornado of snarling fury. She stepped back a few feet, swinging her head from side to side, apparently uncertain whether to charge or retreat. I continued firing flares, landing them in front of her to form a line between the bear and Charlie and me. But it was Charlie who held the bear's attention. Consumed by rage, he snapped and snarled at the end of his lead. I reached down, ready to release him, but the bear stopped and looked back at her cubs.

As if detecting some silent signal, they ran to her as she circled to the left. I fired more flares as she tried to find a way to rush past a ferocious Charlie. Then she stopped, and for a long moment, stared hard at him. Seeing him as a threat, she turned and left, traveling north with her two cubs trotting behind her, their snow-white coats contrasting with their mother's pale cream-colored fur.

The whole episode had lasted only minutes, but had seemed years long. Although this first bear encounter made my heart race, and raw fear had threatened to engulf me, my confidence in my ability to travel safely to the Pole soared to new heights. Charlie had reacted far beyond my expectations. He had saved me from a certain attack, and it was clear that he would defend me with his life if necessary. Charlie, his job done, hardly noticed my tight, grateful embrace. He was still on guard and stood rigid, staring after the bear until she had faded into the far distance. Then, as if nothing out of the ordinary had occurred, he relaxed and returned to lounging in the sun while waiting for me to finish packing. As far as he was concerned, our first polar bear encounter was over and it was time to unwind while I—not so confident—paused now and then to anxiously check the horizons for more bears.

I broke camp, and all went well for the next hour. The sky was clear with just a light wind coming from the north. It was bitterly cold and my blue neoprene mask rapidly developed a thick layer of ice where my breath froze. We had traveled only a couple of miles when, all of a sudden, I noticed movement about four hundred yards away to the southeast. I thought, Oh no, not again! My nerves hadn't recovered from the last bear encounter. Moments later, there was no doubt that it was a bear. It was downwind of us and had probably caught our scent.

I quickly released my skis, grabbed my rifle and flare gun, and stood waiting with Charlie at my side. He was alert, his eyes fixed on the approaching bear, his body rigid and his back hair standing on end, ready for action, but so far remaining silent. I grew anxious. Why didn't he growl or show some aggression toward the newcomer? Perhaps his silence meant that he sensed something I didn't know. So I too stood silent, not moving, with only the sound of my pounding heart in my ears. This bear, a large powerful male, moved toward us at a rapid pace. He held his head low and walked with the typical polar bear pigeon-toed gait. He stopped, raised his black nose, and swung his head slowly back and forth to check our scent, then lowered his head and walked onward again. Charlie, now at the end of his lead, stood silent except for an occasional short, low growl. Soon the bear stood only about 250 feet away and still Charlie remained silent, while I was terrified that this bear, judging by his determined stride, might not stop. The bear quickly closed to 150 feet. I fired one rifle shot overhead and then switched to firing flares in quick succession, but still the bear continued onward. Charlie strained at the end of his lead, growling, while I fired several flares in quick succession, but the bear seemed to have no intention of stopping. I reached for Charlie's collar to set him loose. My thumb was on the collar clip when suddenly Charlie leaped high to the end of his lead with an ear-splitting, snarling growl. Immediately stopping in his tracks, the bear took one long hard look at Charlie, and as I fired more flares, slowly retreated to our left. Once more, Charlie stood silent while we watched the bear move away in a wide sweeping arc, looking back over his shoulder now and then as if reluctant to leave. Although it was clear that the bear was impressed by Charlie's aggressive attitude, I was worried that the bear's reluctance to leave indicated that he might return. Sure enough, after retreating to about three hundred yards away, he stopped and turned to face us. After a few moments he started back toward us with the same determined gait. *This is too much*, I thought. The pit of my stomach was an ice cube. We had to get rid of this bear somehow. I reached down to Charlie's collar, undecided as to whether I should release him and put him at further risk, or try to shoot to kill. I knew that if I only wounded the bear, our situation could become even more dangerous. The bear was now two hundred yards away. I fired another warning shot, then laid out flares as fast as I could load and pull the flare gun trigger, now more thankful than ever that I had brought with me a large supply. Meanwhile, Charlie was in full vicious attack mode. All at once the bear bent down and touched a red-hot flare with his nose. He instantly tossed his head in the air, rolled on the ice, and leaped to his feet as quick as a cat. Running at a fast pace, he didn't look back. He soon disappeared into a rough area of ice. I was shaking with relief.

Two bear encounters in quick succession had been a test of physical and nervous endurance that I hoped I wouldn't have to repeat. I stopped to regroup and have something to eat and drink. I had a severe case of the shakes and was beginning to wonder if my nerves could stand much more abuse. To reward

Charlie for *his* work, I hugged him and fed him some crackers and peanut butter cups. I marveled at the way he had reacted to the two bears. During the first encounter earlier in the day he was all vicious attack, while he had been less aggressive but no less determined when faced by the second bear. I realized that he had an ability to sense what he needed to do and how aggressive he needed to be. There was much for me to learn out here. Charlie leaned on my leg, begging for more crackers. I didn't have much of an appetite. I felt as if I had just survived a head-on collision with a freight train. I gave Charlie my crackers. He certainly had no problem with *his* appetite. To him this polar bear business was fun.

It was already one P.M., and due to bear confrontations, we had covered only two miles. So far, we had seen several white Arctic foxes. I was fascinated by the sheer boldness they displayed as they scurried around so close to the two bears we had seen. They appeared to have no fear. Charlie did not share my interest. Even when we stopped for a snack and they darted in and out around us, close to where Charlie sat, he hardly glanced in their direction. He regarded them as inferior creatures, so he ignored them as if they didn't exist. After gobbling down his treat he lounged back against my sled to enjoy a brief respite as I took extra time to make some adjustments to my loaded sled. As he dozed, a particularly bold fox carefully approached Charlie's tail, which perhaps seemed an interesting object to be investigated. The daring fox was only inches away from the tempting tail when Charlie suddenly noticed the intruder. He leaped to his feet, snapping in total outrage at the sheer audacity of this inferior varmint. The fox, with a high-pitched squeak, leaped a foot in the air and wisely dashed to the safety of a nearby low ice ridge. Even though the fox disappeared in seconds, Charlie continued to stare after it with an attitude of indignation for some time, even as we continued on our way. The whole affair had rattled his pride.

After weaving our way through rough ruble ice, we arrived at an area of high mounds and even higher pinnacles of ice that would provide perfect cover for bears. Emotionally drained from the day's events, I dreaded entering the area, but it lay only three hundred yards ahead and there was no way to avoid the challenge. I set a course straight ahead and hoped for the best. I thought of the many stories I had heard of bears silently stalking hunters who had no idea a bear was close by until they were suddenly attacked. I laid my hand on Charlie's broad back to give myself a measure of self-assurance. He strode ahead with an alert confidence. As an animal born and raised amid snow and ice, he knew instinctively what was going on around him. In contrast, I was only an ignorant visitor in this harsh unforgiving place. Here, there was no room for mistakes! It wasn't long before we entered an icy forest of high jagged mounds and towering fifteen-foot pinnacles. Zigzagging my way through, I searched for the easiest path. My nerves were on edge. The ice platform that Charlie and I traveled across was on the move and sounded like a living being. Tired groans and long high-pitched squeaks came from the depths of the ice as broken edges forced their way past each other, frequently interrupting the deep silence. From time to time, rifle-like cracks exploded through the ice. Now and then, car-sized blocks toppled across our path with a crash. Charlie showed no reaction. He walked as one born to a life of snow and ice, to whom traveling across a moving ice platform that covered the ocean depths was nothing new.

The meteorological office at Resolute had told me before I left that satellite photos showed wide areas of rough ice along my intended route. Fall and early winter storms affect the way the ice sets up. Ice conditions change from year to year. Some years the ice is quite smooth, with fewer areas of challenging rough ice. This year's rougher ice could not only increase the difficulty of travel, but also hide a stalking bear.

Later, we stopped for a snack and Charlie immediately directed his full attention to the day's snack-bag. His formidable skills in the art of persuasion were truly impressive. He had already made it known that peanut butter cups combined with a liberal helping of crackers were a favorite. At first, I paid little heed to his tactics, but he persisted. When I refused and turned away, a look of pained bewilderment came over him. I soon learned that it was easier to share than be subjected to a dog who took on the sad role of one who was being treated in the cruelest way. His tactics were quite straightforward and extremely effective: *Just sit there with a pitiful starving expression as she eats each mouthful. Eventually she'll give in and hand you a generous share of crackers and peanut butter cups.* It was clear, even at this early stage of the expedition, that Charlie knew how to get exactly what he wanted. Sometimes I was left wondering just who was in charge of this journey. Thankfully, he didn't like walnuts, so I at least had them to myself.

After our break I stepped up our pace, and with Charlie walking in his usual place close at my right side, we wove our way through, searching for openings that I could pull my larger sled through. After squeezing our way through a particularly narrow gap, Charlie came to an abrupt stop and fixed his gaze on something ahead of us. With low growls he stepped to the front as if to protect me. At first, I saw only uneven ice ahead, but moments later I thought I detected a slight movement two hundred feet to the front and a little to the right. I needed no further warning. Grabbing my rifle and flare gun, I stared ahead, my heart pounding, still unable to get a clear view of what had moved. Charlie stared in the direction of a car-sized block, and then I saw the bear. It was a male, much smaller than the last, almost hidden behind a barrier of chaotic ice. Then, apparently to get a closer look at us, the bear stepped out into the open. A berserk Charlie charged to the end of his lead as the bear circled to get downwind of us. I fired several flares, but the bear was more intimidated by Charlie, and cautiously stayed back. I had some anxious moments when I lost sight of the bear as he disappeared behind large chunks of ice, but he always reappeared. It looked as if he was moving around to catch our scent so that he could figure out what we were. Many anxious minutes later, the bear, perhaps more curious than aggressive, turned away and ambled off to the south. Now I worried that he might circle around to stalk us from behind. After numerous uneasy glances over my shoulder to check on his whereabouts, I convinced myself that he had left for good. No sooner had I settled into a steady walking cadence than Charlie abruptly spun to the rear. With an ear-splitting growl, he leaped to the end of his lead, almost pulling me off my feet. Regaining my balance, I saw the bear standing motionless, only fifty feet away. Amid Charlie's snarling growls, I fired handfuls of flares in quick succession. After several landed almost at his feet, he apparently decided that it would be more prudent to leave. Moments later he had disappeared, this time for good. I imagined that he might have been glad to be rid of us, especially Charlie. Perhaps he would have been surprised to learn that the feeling was mutual. Once more Charlie had done his job well, and we were safe.

Meeting three bears in one day had left me emotionally exhausted. *This is getting ridiculous,* I thought. During my planning for the expedition, I had expected that being alone and on foot, I stood a good chance of meeting bears—but three in one day had been far beyond my expectation. Bears in these numbers every day would increase our chances of meeting one that would not stop even in the face of Charlie's vigorous attack. Now more concerned than ever, I resolved to ski until we found a place to camp with a clear view in all directions, giving Charlie a better chance of warning me. Ahead and over to the east, there was smooth ice that had escaped the crushing and grinding forces of the moving ice pack. I stopped in the middle and looked about. This would do. Charlie had clear visibility for at least two hundred yards in all directions. I settled him for the night with his pan full of dog food and placed his sled so that it would protect him from the drifting, cold north wind. The thermometer read minus 41 degrees, a little warmer than the previous night. It was close to five o'clock and the sun was sliding down over the western edge of Bathurst Island to leave us bathed in a cold gray light. We had traveled only three miles on this long, nerve-wracking day.

Sitting on my sled sheltered behind my tent, eating my bowl of rice and drinking a cup of hot chocolate, I thought about my predicament. It is one thing to be a member of an expedition of several people, but very different and infinitely more difficult to take a journey like this alone and especially on foot when there is no way to speedily escape danger. I knew beyond a doubt that the Inuit were right: I was far more vulnerable to bear attacks because I was traveling at a slower pace on foot and alone than if I had gone by faster dogsled. And clearly, the many warnings I had received that traveling on foot and alone would attract more bears was true. Rifle shots were a waste of time, I had learned. They sounded too much like the frequent cracking sounds that erupted from the depths of the ice pack. The flare gun, though, had proven to be a definite deterrent. And of course, there was Charlie. He was the main reason we had remained safe through all three bear confrontations. His extreme understanding and sensitivity toward the bears had been nothing short of amazing. He instinctively knew what to do, and his savagery was something to behold. Charlie was a powerful bundle of muscle and intelligence and was able to take care of himself when confronted by a bear. Tony had told me, "A dog can't win a head-to-head fight with a polar bear, but a clever dog like Charlie knows how to nip a bear's rear legs and at the same time stay clear of those powerful jaws and claws that can kill." Also, the day's events had taught me that Charlie would lay down his own life to protect me. I looked across to him. He was sound asleep. I realized that Tony's recommendation—that I let Charlie off his lead only as a last resort in the event of a bear actually charging—had been good advice. He had told me, "Charlie will race after a bear any time he sees one. If you let him off his lead any time you see a bear, Charlie's chances of being hurt will increase many times over. Bears sometimes kill dogs." And this day had taught me more about the ultimate deterrent: shoot to kill. I'm not a hunter and, although legally I could shoot a bear in self-defense, it was something I desperately wanted to avoid unless it was the only remaining option. If I succeeded in wounding a bear, my fate would be sealed. Many an Inuit had been killed by a wounded bear. All in all, I now knew that Charlie and my flare gun would get us safely through to the Pole. He was key to my survival on this journey. Optimism flowed through my veins again. I was thankful for my beloved Charlie. I hurried over to him, woke him up, and gave him a heartfelt hug. I was crying. The frustrations of this difficult day were gone and the tears flowed in relief. Then a strange thing happened—my eyelids froze shut. The cold had turned my tears to ice. One more Arctic lesson: no more crying on this expedition.

Gradually, I thawed and scraped the ice on my eyelids away with warm saliva. It occurred to me that this would *not* be a good time for a visit from a polar bear. Fifteen minutes later, after some painful scraping, I could see again. I returned to finish the last of my uneaten dinner but discovered that everything had turned to ice. My appetite had disappeared anyway, so I walked over to Charlie and sat on his sled. Now that the day was over and I had gotten through the emotional struggle of surviving the worst day of my life, it was sheer freedom to, at least briefly, sit and relax. Charlie laid his big black head on my lap. I stroked his silky black ears and talked about the journey and what might lie ahead of us. I talked about my fear of polar bears, but his only reply was the soft sound of his gentle snores. He had fallen asleep on my lap. Apparently, sleep was of paramount importance, and discussion of bears and our future would have to wait. Having lost the attention of my companion, I glanced at my watch. It was almost time for my eight P.M. scheduled radio call to base camp.

Then I finally slid into my sleeping bag thankful to end the day. The ice was silent, the sun had long since disappeared over Bathurst Island, and the cold gray light of the Arctic night lay over our camp. At eleven o'clock a light dusk settled over us. It was still almost light enough to read. Twenty-four-hour light was fast approaching. By two A.M., the somber gray blanket began to lift, replaced by the pale, soft gray of early morning. Still listening for bears, I finally drifted off to an uneasy sleep.

Early next morning we set out to make up for time lost dealing with bears and rough ice. Although more uneven ice lay ahead, there was an easy route around the mounds, and the gaps between the tall pillars of ice were wider, which allowed our sleds to slide through without jamming. Suddenly Charlie let out a bloodcurdling yelp. My heart jumped and I spun around, thinking that a bear had overtaken us. But I quickly realized that I had stepped on his paw with my sharp steel-edged ski. He held his paw aloft as if to say, "Look what you did." I gently took it in my hand and examined it to make sure the ski's sharp edge hadn't cut it. Seeing no cut, I rubbed the paw. "I'm sorry, Charlie," I said. Apparently, my apology produced a miraculous healing, because he rallied quickly and walked onward without the slightest sign of a limp.

Later, about a half-mile ahead, a maze of mounds and pillars appeared to end at a long east-to-west ridge of ice. It was a pressure ridge stretching snake-like for ten miles, about ten to fifteen feet high, all the way from Bathurst Island to Kalivik Island. Pressure ridges form when the leading edges of ice floes, or bodies of ice, collide under tremendous pressure, crumpling and grinding upward to form jumbled, jagged ridges of car-sized blocks of ice that balance precariously on each other. I hadn't expected to find a ridge of this size in this area, but the changing ice pack is unpredictable. Here the ridge appeared to be at its highest, which was about halfway between the two islands. Off in the distance the ridge looked lower, but it would take a long detour to find a lower crossing. I decided to look for a gap closer by in the wall of ice.

We crossed the tracks of a large male bear amid some fresh tiny tracks of a fox. I saw no sign of the owners, so I nervously kept going. An excited Charlie pressed his black nose to the tracks and tried to follow them. I pulled back on his lead, but Charlie had other ideas. The whole episode quickly developed into a tug-of-war, but I gained ground when I shouted, "No, Charlie, we're supposed to avoid bears, not go find them." He conceded with a look of dour resignation, making it abundantly clear that he was disappointed at my lack of any sense of fun and adventure. As we approached the pressure ridge, I still saw no real gaps. We passed more bear and fox tracks, which led to a large blood-spattered area where a bear had killed a seal, which now lay partly eaten on the ice. Charlie gleefully pulled me closer. I gave in and joined in the investigation. It had been a ringed seal breathing hole, and the unfortunate occupant had met a violent end. A delighted Charlie eagerly chewed the few leftover seal carcass scraps, but when he rolled on the bloodstained ice, I quickly stopped him. A dog that smelled like a seal would attract bears rather than deter them. And there might be more seal breathing holes around the pressure ridge—undoubtedly good hunting for bears. If that was true, this was definitely a place I wanted to leave as soon as possible. "Charlie, let's get out of here before you smell like a seal and attract every bear in the Arctic." His whole attitude radiated outrage. *Here is food just lying there ready to be consumed, and she expects me to move on without taking advantage of such a bounty!* After a few more strong tugs on his lead, he consented to follow, but he made it clear that it was against his better judgment.

I headed to our right, where I saw a ramp of hard-packed snow reaching halfway up the pressure ridge. On each side of the snow ramp the tortured, fractured ice was piled in an uneven mass of car-sized blocks, some as large as six feet or more across. Leaving my skis behind, I climbed the ramp, looking for a way over the top. At the top, four feet of unstable, broken ice still had to be crossed. The only thing to do was to chop a path over the top, pull my sled up by hand, and then lower it carefully down the other side. Next, I turned my attention to Charlie's sled, which, being smaller and lighter, was an easier task. Then it was Charlie's turn to scramble up the ridge. He effortlessly jumped from block to block with the ease of a skilled gymnast and joined me on the other side. Clear of the pressure ridge, it was sheer joy to ski over the smoothest surface we had so far encountered. We made good mileage, with no bears or open water in sight.

At four-thirty the mileage wheel attached to the back of my sled registered only five miles. All that work for so little gain. To make matters worse, I could see more rough ice ahead. Charlie and I were the only expedition going to the magnetic North Pole this year, so I hadn't been able to get any snow and ice reports of what lay ahead of us. Pilots flying north, and Bezal at base camp had already warned me that the ice was rougher this year, with more open water leads. Bezal also warned of high winds, describing my route to the Pole as a "wind tunnel." Thankfully, so far high winds had not been a problem.

Desperate to cover more miles, I continued onward. Another pressure ridge crossed our path, this one only three or four feet high with long easy gaps between the blocks of ice. "This is more our size, Charlie," I said as we headed toward the first gap. On the other side, all I could see stretching in all directions was a wide area of broken, jumbled ice. The sun, low in the sky, spread a golden glow over the western sides of tall pinnacles of ice that cast long, dark, ghostlike shadows to the east. A fog of golden crystals spread softly over the coast of nearby Bathurst Island. The scene before me was unreal, unearthly. A photograph could never capture the beauty of a land and icescape untouched and uncomplicated by humans. Standing next to Charlie, I was hesitant to enter those silent dark shadows that I knew could be an ideal place for a hidden polar bear to stalk us. To add to my worries, Charlie had been sniffing the air to the east for the last half hour. I saw nothing—but was there a bear out there? Or was it just the scent of a seal? As I stood leaning on my ski poles, I decided that worrying about what might happen wasn't going to improve our mileage. The only way was ahead and I had to hope for better conditions on the other side. I charged ahead and didn't stop until we had escaped the shadowed area. We pressed on for another two miles before making camp. Meanwhile, Charlie still kept looking east. It had me worried. What was he looking for? If it was a bear, could it be keeping abreast of us? So far, I had no way of knowing. Ahead lay an iceberg about thirty feet high, calved from a distant glacier and trapped in the crushing grasp of the winter ice pack. A wide layer of smooth ice, providing a good camping spot with adequate visibility, surrounded it.

The sun had quietly slipped away and the temperature was dropping, although it was still in the minus thirties. I fed Charlie and went to work setting up camp. But Charlie seemed uneasy. He ate a little of his food, but left the rest in his pan as he stood looking east into the distance. Something was bothering him. Even after the long day, he didn't sit or lie down. I stared through the gray light, but could see nothing. I was worried. *Surely there must be a bear out there,* I thought, *or why would Charlie leave his food and be on guard?* Sleep was out of the question until I discovered what was out there. Wearing my big down parka,

I sat on my sled with my flare gun and rifle at my side and wrote the day's events in my journal. The cold had frozen my pen, so I used one of the many pencils I had brought with me. My severely suffering hands made writing difficult, but although the writing looked crude, at least it was readable.

Suddenly Charlie growled softly. Dropping the journal, I grabbed my rifle and flare gun and stood at his side. I saw nothing, but as Charlie's growls grew louder, I noticed movement to one side of some blocks of ice the size of a Volkswagen Beetle. And there, about two hundred yards away, an adult male bear stepped out from where he had been hidden from my view and walked toward us. As the bear closed in, Charlie, with bared teeth, strained and leaped at the end of his lead. The bear hesitated, apparently fazed by Charlie's aggressive leaping and snarling, and turned south as if to leave. And then he stopped, turned, and again moved toward us. Now Charlie was beside himself with rage. Finally, the bear, apparently re-thinking his situation, turned away for a final time and headed south at a fast lope. Judging by Charlie's watchful attitude throughout the day, I was sure that this bear had been following us at a distance all day long, but now, in the face of Charlie's defensive attitude, he had decided an attack would be unwise. His best strategy was to leave us alone. With the disappearance of the bear, Charlie finally relaxed, finished his dinner, and, with a contented sigh, curled up and fell fast asleep even before I could give him a goodnight hug. Once again, I was thankful for him and relieved beyond words. How I wished I could figure out these bears and understand their intentions as Charlie did. It was eleven o'clock. The pale light of a full moon sparkled across the ice. Confident that we had seen the last of the curious bear, I climbed into my sleeping bag for my best night's sleep on the journey so far.

On the prowl

Chapter Five — *Bear Attack!*

According to my map, eleven miles ahead was a fifteen-mile-wide bay called Goodsir Inlet. The Inuit had warned me that this was a well-known bear hunting area due to its abundant seal population. Considering that we had already had more than enough trouble from bears, I couldn't wait to put it behind us. The very name of the place made me nervous. Occasionally we walked across seal lairs hollowed out deep in the ice and concealed by a layer of surface snow. With his sensitive nose, Charlie had caught the scent of the seals and their newborn pups hidden in the lairs, and would immediately investigate, using his front paws like backhoes as he dug at a frantic pace straight down through the ice to the lair. I had pulled him away, concerned that if Charlie found a seal, its scent would attract a bear. I had been told that bears traveling downwind could detect seal scent as much as twenty miles away. Departing in haste, I'd paid little heed to Charlie's complaints. He had left with the gloomiest of looks and at first lagged behind to protest my disrespect toward the sport of seal hunting. I wouldn't have been surprised if he was remembering back to his earlier days, when his polar bear and seal hunting were encouraged. As the day progressed, a northerly fifteen-mile-per-hour wind sent fine snow sliding toward us across the ice surface. Charlie's face developed a thin mask of ice, but it seemed not to bother him. After all, he was born and raised in these conditions, so I'm sure he accepted them as normal. The thick fur coat that covered even his face prevented the ice crystals from reaching his skin. But I had no such protection. My face mask soon iced up, causing the neoprene to stick to my skin, and I had to squint through my frozen eyelashes to search for a way through and around obstacles. I tried rubbing the ice off my eyelashes, but soon gave up the losing battle. I was learning to accept these things as normal. Now and then we crossed bear tracks of various sizes, but one was gigantic, measuring almost a foot across. "I hope we don't meet the bear that fits into those tracks," I told Charlie.

The jagged teeth of the sharp wind bit into my body, even though the sun shone. We were making good progress according to the mileage counter on my sled. It was only noon and already we had traveled seven miles. Nevertheless, it was not long before we entered yet another area of uneven, broken, and rutted ice that looked as though a giant had thrown chunks and blocks in all directions. I was heartily fed up with the constant need to find a reasonable route through the jumble that at times forced me to take my harness off and pull both my sled and Charlie's through narrow gaps by hand. At ten miles into the day's trek, I hoped I would gain a better view ahead and find smoother ice. The nearby coast of Bathurst rose over one hundred feet, making it a good place for a wide view. From there I hoped to see a way around the tortured area that surrounded us. I veered in that direction.

Soon, the thin, fragile coastal ice creaked and moved beneath my skis as I headed toward a convenient snow ramp that led up from the sea ice to a flat ledge on the ice-covered land about fifty feet above the coastline. I hauled my sled up by hand, while Charlie followed close behind. The narrow ledge barely accommodated both sleds, so I pulled and scrambled up another twenty-five feet to a wider ledge. The higher I went, the stronger the wind blew and tore at my clothes. A better vantage point, from which I would be able to see the route ahead, lay much higher. The bitterly cold wind cut deep into my body and convinced me to leave Charlie with the two sleds on the ledge while I hurried upward to get the best possible view. I had gone only a few feet when I was stopped in my tracks by a loud mournful howl behind me. With muzzle raised to the heavens, Charlie let me know in no uncertain terms that he did not appreciate being left behind. Feeling guilty, I hurried downward and released him. He immediately jumped on me, rolled on the ice, and then jumped on me again. He seemed happy to be on land, was in a playful mood, and wanted me to join in. His heavy body knocked me down twice. Picking myself up, I shouted to him to stop and told him, "Charlie, I've had all the joy I can stand." I scrambled up the slope with a delighted Charlie leading the way in great leaping bounds, his thick fur coat protecting him from the wind. At the top a glorious sight greeted me. About a mile offshore I was relieved to see longer stretches of flatter ice, to the east and to the north, which lay between extensive chaotic areas. Eager to escape the increasingly cold wind, Charlie and I returned to the sleds and I slid them both down to the coast and out onto the ice.

Charlie, still in a playful mood, bounded with joyful leaps down the slope and stood waiting on the ice for me to join him. His romp on land had invigorated him and he was still in a playful mood. The cold wind didn't faze him, but I was shivering. I reasoned that if I set a brisk pace I would soon warm up. Drawn by the promise of easier ice ahead, Charlie and I set out at a pace that I hoped would warm me, but I still shivered. It was minus 34 degrees, and the twenty-mile-per-hour wind had dropped the wind-chill temperature to minus 85 degrees. The cold knifed through my clothes. I skied hard until I was a mile offshore and finally on the smooth ice I had seen from my vantage point on the island. Even though it was only three P.M., it was time to camp and warm up. I reasoned that in the morning I could start fresh, push hard to reach the other side of Goodsir Inlet in one day and leave the bear hunting area behind.

I decided to visit Charlie once more before bedtime. Calling his name, I walked over to him. He raised his head briefly, opened his sleepy eyes, and then tucked his nose under his tail. *Well,* I thought, *not much conversation here. I might as well go to sleep myself.* I patted him goodnight and returned to the tent. The wind had dropped and a clear sky arched above us. It was a clear evening, and again I marveled at my good fortune with the weather. Tomorrow's weather looked promising too.

Next morning, we set out on a windless, minus 51-degree early morning to tackle the smoother ice floes, slabs of pancake-shaped ice that cover the Arctic Ocean. Some are several hundred feet wide, surrounded by rougher ice caused by the pressuring and collision of the ice floe edges. We were making good time, skirting some larger mounds of ice over fifteen feet high that were sprinkled here and there. We crossed over several cracks in the ice, some only a hair's width and others perhaps six inches across. Charlie didn't like to cross the wider ones. He always hesitated, but followed in response to a sharp tug on his lead. He was afraid of falling into the water. I wondered if an Arctic dog instinctively has respect for the cold, chilling waters, knowing that a dip can be fatal.

It was close to ten A.M., almost time for a quick snack. There was a larger hummock of ice ahead about twenty feet high, shaped and smoothed like a weathered iceberg. Although reluctant to stop at all, I knew it was important to eat regularly to keep a good energy level, so I decided to stop on the other side. Just as we were about to veer around one side Charlie stopped, then uttered a deep growl, his back hair standing on end. His growls warned me that a bear, still unseen, was behind the iceberg. In an instant I released my skis, unclipped the sled-hauling ropes from my harness, grabbed my rifle and flare gun, and stood waiting with Charlie. He was straining at the end of his lead, snarling and staring at the wall of ice. Every nerve in my body was on edge, fearful of what would happen next. I had not long to wait. Suddenly, the largest male bear I had so far seen stepped out from behind the ice, paused momentarily, then raced past me and with a massive front paw flipped my sled over as though it were a tiny toothpick. Then the bear, only twenty feet away, reared up on his hind legs, dwarfing me as I stood there. Charlie's growls were deafening. My right thumb pressed down on the clip on his collar, instantly releasing him. With lightning speed, Charlie raced to the bear, grabbed his right rear heel, and hung on. I fired a rifle shot point blank at the bear, but as he twisted down and around with mouth agape, trying to rid his heel of a wildly ferocious Charlie, the bullet flew harmlessly overhead. In his desperate efforts to shake off his tormentor, the bear reared again and reached back with teeth and claws, trying to grab Charlie. With each turn Charlie swung his body away, his powerful jaw still gripping that white furry heel. Now desperate to free himself, the bear swung again and tore loose from Charlie's steely grip. He raced to freedom across the ice while Charlie, in a frenzy of enthusiasm and speed, sprinted in hot pursuit. This was the bear chase of his dreams.

Glad to be alive, I stood watching both disappear. They quickly became two steadily diminishing dots in the white glare of the vast emptiness, and my world grew silent. But my relief was short-lived. Charlie was gone. Would he come back? Would the bear turn and injure him? This was to be a day that would live long in memory. I recalled Tony's words. He had told me before we left that if I let Charlie off his lead to chase a bear, I might not see him again. "He loves to chase bears and might run so far that he could be injured or even killed by another bear that could be prowling nearby." I desperately searched the horizon for any sign of Charlie, but saw none. I had no idea where I might search for him in the vast emptiness that had swallowed them both. My mind raced frantically with questions but no answers. A few moments ago, I had never been so afraid in my life, but now I felt numb. I walked around to keep warm, stretching my gaze into the distance, hoping to see Charlie. It would do no good to go out to look for him. Where would I look in all that blank space? At that point, it was impossible to consider what I would do if he didn't return. I couldn't imagine having to go on without Charlie— although I knew that if he didn't return, I would have to finish the journey without him. Worse still, I couldn't think of the awful possibility of not taking my buddy home. I stood there, disconsolate, with a growing concern that I might have seen Charlie for the last time. A long half hour later, when I was almost at my wits' end with worry, I saw a tiny black dot in the far distance. I prayed, *Lord, please let this be Charlie.* Then I realized that of course it was Charlie. He was the only black thing out there. I was overwhelmed with relief as he raced back to where I waited, his tongue hanging out and a happy doggy smile on his face. I ran to meet him and hugged him tight. To celebrate having survived the bear attack, and of course to honor Charlie's first-rate bear chase, I took a few peanut butter cups and crackers out of the day's snack bag and together we feasted.

The whole encounter had seemed to last a lifetime. My hands were still shaking. If it had not been for Charlie, I might not have survived. In contrast, Charlie had stopped panting from his long run and had enjoyed the whole event. To him this was fun. He had shown no fear. He was on his mettle. It had perhaps been the most wonderful bear chase of his life.

After I turned my sled right side up again, I gathered and loaded my scattered gear. Luckily, everything had survived without damage. I skied past the iceberg and found the remains of a large seal. Apparently, we had interrupted the bear's meal and he hadn't appreciated it. His attack was his way of showing his extreme displeasure. A delighted Charlie immediately leaped on the carcass. So soon after his preventing the bear's attack, I didn't have the heart to stop him. I reasoned that just once he should have his way with a seal carcass. After a few minutes of watching him tear into the flesh with wild enthusiasm, though, it occurred to me that the unhappy bear might return to finish his meal, and if he found us there with the carcass, he could become unstoppable. "Charlie," I said, "let's get out of here."

Charlie steadfastly refused to leave his newfound treasure. He tried to drag the seal with him. For my part, I tried to reason with him. But he was undaunted in his determination that the seal had to come with us. From his point of view, the seal was his and that was that! His day had been an amazing success. First a most rewarding bear chase, and now a seal carcass to claim as his own.

I tried to pull the seal away, but Charlie just clung on. Now I was really worried that we had been there too long, possibly giving the bear time to return. We had to leave *now!* With renewed resolve, I pulled hard on his lead. At first, he was deaf to my commands and urgent tugs on his lead, but I could see his resolve weakening. Nursing an air of grievance at what he thought was my total indifference to his culinary needs, he reluctantly agreed to depart, but only with frequent looks back at the treasure he was being forced to leave behind. Even when the seal lay far behind us, Charlie continued to let me know that my behavior and lack of consideration of his needs were crimes not to be forgotten. It was evening before he forgave me.

We hurried across the inlet, continuing nonstop until we welcomed the relatively smooth ice highway ahead of us. Through the afternoon glare I saw a tall slender pillar of ice standing alone in the far distance. It was in line with our route, so I aimed for it. At least thirty feet high, the pillar was white, streaked with pale blue, a graceful ice sculpture. Stopping to take a photo, I arranged my sled and Charlie in front of the pinnacle and set my camera on the tripod. With the timer set, I ran to stand at Charlie's side. With my mask off, I smiled at the camera, but there was no click. The camera had frozen again. The joys of Arctic photography! After a few more tries I gave up, and took a photo of Charlie by himself.

At five o'clock, with the sun setting, I could see Rapid Point jutting out from Bathurst Island on the far side of the inlet. The ice-covered land was so flat I could hardly tell where the land stopped and the sea ice began. We traveled out and around the point into a haunting, desolate, lonely moonscape. Strong sea currents swept around the point. Huge plates of ice confronted us, some a hundred feet wide, that had lifted up onto each other. Other plates had ridden over the top of their neighbors, leaving their sharp edges pointing skyward. The ice creaked and groaned as it protested the abuse it was being dealt from the ocean currents. I kept to the less angled plates, but my skis still slid sideways to the bottom. Charlie didn't like it at all. There were too many cracks and wider gaps in the ice for his liking. But we kept going until the ice flattened. It wasn't safe to camp on the unstable ice near those swift currents, and I was glad to get away from that lonely, ghostly place. It was six o'clock by the time we stopped. The day had been long and emotionally exhausting. More than anything, I wanted to get into my sleeping bag and go to sleep to give my mind some relief. Charlie was happier now that we were on more stable ice, but he was tired. As soon as we stopped, he curled up and went to sleep, even before eating his dinner. He too had had a long day. It was hard work chasing bears and protecting me. He didn't wake up until I had cooked dinner. Then he was ready to eat. To reward him for his day's work and to make up for forcing him to leave the seal behind, I gave him a pan of rice and an extra ration of his food, coupled with his favorite crackers. That did the trick. He was a happy fellow. All was well again and I had been forgiven for my earlier transgression over the seal. I slid into my sleeping bag and slept soundly, without a single dream about bears.

After the bear encounter I hugged Charlie tight

Crack in the ice-covered Arctic Ocean

Chapter Six —
Ice Breakup, Open Water

A well-rested Charlie was up and ready for breakfast. He had slept with his back to the wind, and his thick coat was crusted with a layer of snow. I never got used to seeing him lie on the bare snow and ice with no shelter. The High Arctic is a cold desert with very little snowfall. There is rarely enough snow to provide insulation against the brutal cold and wind for these hardy dogs. They are used as tools to pull heavy Inuit sleds, they exist on a diet of seal meat, and when water is not available in the frozen darkness of winter, they eat ice. When not working, they are chained outside, even in the extremes of winter weather. Their thick fur coats and hardy souls give the words *endurance* and *survival* a meaning far beyond the imagination of people in more friendly environments.

I woke up and crawled out of my tent to greet the minus 44 degrees that made my body feel brittle with cold. I looked around for polar bears, but the twenty-mile-per-hour wind gusts that whistled over the ice kicked the thin layer of fine snow into the air, cutting visibility down to just a few yards. The rising wind was sweeping in from the north and the skies were clear, but I worried that these strong gusts might be the forerunners of an oncoming weather change. I was irritated at myself for having slept so long. My fingers were swollen and the pain was wretched as I pulled my liner gloves on. Rapid improvement was unlikely given that my hands faced daily abuse when using my stove or even gripping my ski poles as I traveled. Packing my sled was a challenge in the wind, which threatened to blow away anything that wasn't anchored down. At last, we were ready to leave just before noon, our latest start.

The ice ahead was a smooth highway covered by a thin layer of snow and a few hard-packed snowdrifts scattered about. The sky, almost white from the reflecting ice beneath, stretched endlessly overhead to scarcely touch the horizons in all directions. Skiing into the wind with Charlie close at my side, his face covered in a thin layer of ice, I felt dispirited. My hands were a mess, and the wind soon froze my face mask. We needed good mileage today, and I was starting our day at noon. I was grumpy and impatient. A few minutes after we began, Charlie stepped over the right-hand rope leading to the sled, tangling his leash with the rope. It had happened before, but then it had been no problem. We had always untangled in a couple of minutes. But this time I lost my temper and shouted at him, "Stupid dog, use your brains and stop getting tangled up." His reaction was immediate. He cringed, lay down on the ice, and dropped his head onto his paws, looking up at me with sad eyes. My angry voice, which sounded too loud in the surrounding silence, and the sight of a cringing Charlie jerked me to my senses. How could I shout at him like that? I felt ashamed. He had become a loving, faithful friend and had saved my life. It was time to make up. "I'm so sorry, Charlie," I said as I bent down to pat him. The effect was electrifying. He jumped up, licking my gloved hand, waving his tail like a flag of victory. I hugged him tight and resolved that no matter what happened, I would never speak to him like that again. I skied off in a much better frame of mind with a happy Charlie at my side. No more grumpiness. I had learned my lesson!

At three o'clock Charlie and I settled down behind my sled, out of the wind, for a snack. After eating, I tried to put my mask on again, but it was a frozen board. I chopped off some of the ice with my axe, then broke off most of the rest. I was glad to put the mask back on. Although uncomfortable, it stopped my face from freezing.

We had traveled about six miles when Charlie hit on a bright idea. He loved a good back rub, but now he took it to new heights. He discovered that if he pressed in close to my right leg, he would get an automatic side scratch as my leg moved back and forth with each step. At first, I thought, *How cute*, but changed my mind when his ninety-four pounds pressed so hard against my leg that he sent me stumbling off balance and I was unceremoniously dumped on the ice in a tangle of legs and skis. Charlie stopped and stared quizzically into my face, probably wondering, *Now what is she doing*? Untangling myself and maneuvering my skis on the slippery ice, I got to my feet, pointed us north again, and set out once more. This expedition might be many things, but it was not boring. Charlie and the polar bears would see to that. Charlie began leaning on me again, so I devised a new ski technique, jerking my right knee out to the side to signal him that he was leaning too hard. We developed a nice but unorthodox rhythm. Eventually, much to my relief, it discouraged his little game.

At six o'clock, we had traveled ten miles—respectable for such a late start with the wind gusting over twenty miles per hour, and visibility no more than two hundred yards. I could hardly see the coast through the blowing snow. The stronger gusts raced by with a loud whistle, dying away in the distance. It was torture putting my tent up. My hands were in bad shape. More blisters had burst during the day as I skied, but I chose not to look at them until I had finished all my camp jobs. If I ignored my hands, they might not feel as bad as they looked. Lighting the stove and cooking dinner felt like one long painful scream.

Common sense told me that I shouldn't take shortcuts with eating and drinking, but I decided that common sense would have to wait until tomorrow. To save my hands, I ate a sparse, cold dinner of odds and ends. Next, I peeled off my inner gloves and was greeted by the sickening sight of bleeding, raw fingers. Although my hands were a serious problem, my bigger worry was whether I could get out of the tent in time to greet a bear. I had no plans to entertain a bear inside.

At nine o'clock the wind, although still strong, seemed to be tearing at the tent walls a little less. I peeked out the door at Charlie. He was curled up fast asleep, sheltered by his sled and the tent. I still felt guilty about having him sleep outside, but I knew it would better enable him to warn me if a polar bear came visiting. I finally fell asleep to the rhythmic flapping of the tent. I awoke at two A.M. listening for the wind. It had died down and everything was quiet and still. Outside it was already light again. When I began this journey, a gray dusk settled over us about eight o'clock at night. Now it was light again at two o'clock. Soon we would have twenty-four hours of daylight, something I looked forward to. I checked on Charlie. He looked peaceful, and I soon fell asleep again.

At daybreak I stepped out of the tent to greet the first rays of sun and clear skies. Seven straight days of clear skies were more than I had expected, given the changeable nature of Arctic weather. The golden rays of the early morning sun were pushing their way through a thin fog of ice crystals. There was just a hint of a halo around the sun. I felt a little uneasy. Did these subtle changes mean a change in weather? I hoped not!

A refreshed Charlie was already awake and ready for his breakfast. He flopped down on his back, white paws in the air, inviting me to scratch his tummy. This did not strike me as a suitable pose for a ferocious polar bear guard dog. Instead, he looked like a big affectionate house pet with nothing better to do than make himself lovable. I knelt and scratched the white blaze that ran from his chest all the way down to his tummy, using my knuckles because my fingers were too sore. He loved it and temporarily floated off to doggy heaven. Hungry after last night's meager dinner, I ate most of two bowls of granola and shared part of the second one with Charlie, much to his delight.

Starting out at six A.M. I noticed that the ice crystal fog had increased in density. With visibility decreasing, I had to strain to see the route ahead, but at least there was no wind. Soon the ice fog grew even denser. The reflected sunlight created a pale golden curtain around us that resembled the finest, softest chiffon. The phenomenon of sunlight and ice crystals had turned this harsh, unforgiving ice desert into an oasis of quiet golden beauty. Skiing slowly, I longed to make the scene last forever. Our sleds slid easily over wide patches of hard-packed, windblown snow. We stopped once when Charlie started to dig straight down, apparently having caught the scent of a seal lair. But moments later, he walked on. Perhaps no one was at home, so it wasn't worth further investigation. A dense fog that totally obscured the distant island coastline crept silently toward us and soon replaced the golden aura of ice crystals. I had been using the coastline as a reference for navigation, but now the fog forced me to follow my shadow. Even with only the slightest hint of a shadow, I could use it for navigation. My watch read eight-thirty A.M. and I was traveling due north. My shadow pointed northwest and would change its angle by fifteen degrees every hour. There was no wind, just an eerie calm. It was impossible to see the route ahead or watch for bears. Charlie would have to let me know. I could still see the faint outline of my shadow, but found myself losing depth perception. In a true whiteout, light coming from all directions has the same strength and casts no shadows. The horizon disappears and space, even close by, has no depth. It is impossible to know where the surface is, and anyone traveling on foot in these conditions stumbles as if the world had dropped away. Cautiously I continued onward, still following my shadow, which continued to fade. I stumbled over unseen chunks of ice. Now and then I collided with Charlie, who showed infinite patience with his companion's unsteady gait. Surely, he must have wondered at my sudden inability to keep to my side of the "road." I stopped. I could see nothing beyond my outstretched arm. I could feel the ice moving beneath our feet, and I could hear long-drawn-out sighs that sounded like skis sliding across the snow.

    Completely spooked, I said to no one in particular, "What in the world's going on?" but then realized it was just the ice making its usual conversation. I remarked to Charlie, "I wonder what would happen if I put my hand out and felt something white, warm, and fuzzy," but immediately pushed the thought away. The soundscape alone was eerie enough, without allowing my imagination to go wild. But then as I stood in our tiny world, I became increasingly concerned that the ice beneath us was moving and making cracking sounds, as if it might be breaking up. We couldn't go ahead because I couldn't see what we might walk into. I wondered if we were headed for open water. Stopping to camp and wait for better visibility wasn't an option because I had no idea if the ice around us was safe enough for a camp. To make matters worse, Charlie began to show the usual cautious signs he would normally display when close to water. How close and how stable was the ice we were standing on? The ice was a grayish color. I tested it with my pole. The pointed end penetrated the ice fairly easily, but didn't quite reach water. That, combined with the color, meant that we were on thin ice and salt water wasn't far beneath our feet. I dared not move forward into an unknown that I couldn't see. All I could do was hope the wind would return to get rid of the fog. Charlie became increasingly agitated and pulled back on his lead, wanting to go back the way we had come. Did this mean that we were on the edge of open water? I decided to follow him and go back at least a few paces while I watched his reaction. About twenty or so yards back he seemed to settle down. Now I knew there must be water ahead. I decided to follow my tracks back until I could find thicker ice. After we had backtracked perhaps as much as a quarter of a mile, I tested the ice with my ski pole. It seemed thicker and wasn't the same gray color of the ice up ahead. Charlie seemed at ease, so I decided to stay there and wait for better visibility.

Two long hours later, a light wind drifted in. It was enough to start clearing out the impenetrable fog. Anxiously, I stared ahead. It took some time to see any definition in the snow and ice. Eventually I thought I could see a dark area up ahead, but I still wasn't sure. A short while later there was no doubt that I was looking ahead to a wide gap in the ice. In the dense whiteout conditions, we had almost taken a dip in the ocean. I was puzzled because I hadn't expected open water this early. But I had been warned that this wasn't a normal ice year. No wonder Charlie had been nervous. He hated water and it scared him. He couldn't have seen through the fog—he must have somehow sensed it. That's why he wanted to go back the way we had come. Now that I knew what lay ahead of us, we would wait for improved visibility to find a route around the danger.

It was about one P.M. before the fog thinned and the improved visibility allowed us to move forward. I followed our previous tracks ahead and to my horror discovered that we had stopped only about twenty feet from the edge of ice that had split apart, forming a gap about ten feet wide. Charlie had sensed water ahead and we had retreated to safety. No doubt Charlie, during a lifetime spent in the Arctic, had learned to sense water before actually seeing it. He knew of the dangers of falling in. Not only did he warn me of polar bears, but now he had warned me of an unseen, watery danger ahead. The break stretched east to west, and the ice around the break was thin and fragile. We traveled about a mile before skirting the eastern edge of the open water to reach safety on the other side. Happy to be free of water and thin ice, Charlie and I stepped up the pace in the improved visibility. The ice smoothed and we made good time for the next five miles. Looking westward, I noticed that the island's coast had flattened out to a low plain, which I knew was called Airstrip Point. I could only imagine how this place got its name. Perhaps some thankful pilot had found a flat landing spot when he needed it most.

Before the sun dipped in the west, I set up camp. In spite of the fog and ice conditions, we had traveled eleven miles. Temperatures had warmed to minus 31 degrees, a ten-degree increase since seven that morning. A light north wind whispered by the tent, barely moving the fabric. The fog was gone and I could see clearly in all directions. Were the day's weather changes the harbingers of a storm from the south? Because I felt so uneasy about the weather, I tied the tent down with two extra ice screws just in case the wind picked up. I fed Charlie. After eating he would normally lie down to sleep about twenty feet away from the tent, where I had anchored his lead so that he could get a clear view of any approaching bear. But now, with a lot of yipping and whining, he begged to sit beside me as I cooked. I knew it wasn't companionship he sought. His main interest was my upcoming dinner. I gave in and allowed him to come closer. We would disregard his bear-watching duties, at least for now. He lay down with his head on his paws, and his two brown eyes followed my every move. As soon as I began eating my bowl of rice he immediately stood, expecting to receive his share. *Here we go again*, I thought, *that begging look*. I placed two spoons full of rice in front of him. It was gone in a flash. I turned my back, hoping to finish my meal in peace, but halfway through my eyes turned in Charlie's direction as if pulled by a magnet. He had reached toward me as far as his lead would allow, and his two eyes were an inch from mine. The message in those eyes was clear: *Won't you share just a little more?* It was of course impossible to refuse, so I gave him half of what was left. I even sprinkled a little of his beloved milk powder on top, and then added a few crackers on the side for dessert. But Charlie wasn't ready to limit his ambition to just sharing food. When I tried to lead him to his place twenty feet away from the tent, he pulled back. It was clear that he wanted to sleep inside. *This is just too much*, I thought. *If we don't maintain some reasonable degree of discipline on this journey, we might never get there at all.* "Come on, Charlie, let's go," I told him. After settling a disappointed Charlie outside the tent, I took one last look around for bears and crawled into the tent.

The dawn came gray and somber. The wind that had been only a whisper during the night had increased to a gusting ten miles per hour. Worried that a major storm was on its way, I hurried to break camp, pack, and leave by seven o'clock. Even though a southerly wind could bring a storm, the wind, now at our backs, felt good. Charlie didn't complain when we traveled into a headwind, but I did. My face mask turned into a cold, uncomfortable sheet of inch-thick ice, my eyelashes froze, and worse still, I had to be careful that my eyes didn't freeze when I couldn't wear my goggles because of fogging. It was important to wear them as much as possible, but when fog froze on the lenses, I had to take them off to watch for bears, which left my eyes unprotected from the wind. But now a welcome tailwind blew a thin layer of snow along the surface of the ice in long fingers that silently led our way north. Behind me, my ski tracks vanished as soon as they were formed. Ahead I could see the high coastal cliffs stretching into the distance. In places they rose two hundred feet, almost straight up out of the ice-covered sea. A thick layer of ice covered the cliff tops to resemble the glistening white frosting on a cake. Each ledge held an icy frosting, while exposed rock was a pale sandy color. The jagged cliffs were a dramatic contrast to the flat lowlands we had left behind us.

At ten o'clock, in an increasing wind, an enormous wall of blue-black clouds stretched far across the ice to the east and engulfed Bathurst to the west. The wall of clouds was still several miles to the south of us, but it would soon catch up. It was hard to tell how fast the storm was traveling, but I knew we were vulnerable out there, being chased down by a storm of unknown proportions. I stopped to measure the wind speed and temperature. The readings were fifteen miles per hour and minus 21 degrees. The storm was pushing warmer air ahead of it. Everything around us took on a gray, bleak look. Stumbling over the invisible chunks of ice, I saw what looked like a wide area of flat ice ahead, but it seemed far away. The surrounding drab gray light and lack of depth perception made everything seem unreal. I felt uneasy, as if I were the only person in a rapidly shrinking gray world. To regain some measure of reality, I laid my hand on Charlie's broad back. At least he was real. By now visibility and depth perception had virtually disappeared. The leading edge of the storm had caught up with us. It was time to set up camp before the wind grew too strong to erect the tent. Charlie, encrusted with snow, didn't seem to care about the worsening conditions. His four paws hadn't had any problems stepping over and around the chunks of ice that had caused me to stumble.

Facing north, I was unbuckling my sled harness and ready to set up camp when I saw a small animal stepping off the shoreline onto the sea ice. I strained through the gray gloom to figure out what it could be. Charlie was watching with interest, but showed no concern. It was small, so at first I thought it must be an Arctic fox, but even in the gray light with practically no depth perception, it seemed a bit larger. Then it dawned on me. It had to be a bear cub. But where was its mother? As the light suddenly brightened, leading my depth perception to vastly improve, I froze in shock. Only one hundred feet away, a full-grown bear stood staring back at me. With my heart thumping, I slowly inched my way backward to my sled where, without taking my eyes off the bear, I reached behind me and grabbed my flare gun. Until then Charlie had been watchful but showed no aggression. Now, as the bear took a couple of steps toward us, he strained to the end of his leash and softly growled. The bear stopped, then moments later took a couple more steps toward us. She stopped again when Charlie's growls increased in volume. Without another look, the bear turned away and walked off to the north, vanishing into the gray gloom. I stood there motionless for several minutes. Perhaps I was the first human the bear had ever seen, so it was merely curious? That would explain why Charlie chose to send out warning growls rather than a full-scale defense. As for me, my lesson had been well learned. On this journey, I would assume all animals were full-grown bears until proven otherwise. I sensed that Charlie had the bear figured out long before I did. His calm approach perhaps indicated that he was not affected by the lack of depth perception to the degree that I was. Could it be that his canine eyesight was more attuned to these conditions than my human eyesight was?

By three o'clock the storm had grown no worse. The south wind had stabilized at about fifteen miles per hour and the temperature had warmed rapidly to minus 19 degrees. Uncertain how long the storm would last, I chopped several chunks of ice to melt for water and laid them at the tent door within easy reach. Just before ducking into my tent, I went through my usual ritual of a last-minute look around for bears and saw something moving to the south. Through the grayness, I saw the bear. He was coming straight at us with that peculiar pigeon-toed gait, which made him appear to be two moving

Charlie begging for his share

objects side by side in this murky dim light. At 150 feet I fired two warning shots from my rifle over his head with no visible effect, then began shooting flares in front of him as fast as I could pull the trigger. He kept coming at us with a determined gait that meant business. He was a big-boned male, but looked thinner than the others we had so far encountered. That could mean a hungry bear desperate for a meal. When he was about seventy-five feet away, things looked serious. He was walking in a straight line toward us and nothing was turning him away. I fired a couple more flares, thinking I might have to let Charlie off his leash. Then the first flare landed almost on the bear's left front paw, too close for his comfort. He jumped and veered to his right. The next one landed right under his nose, making him jump backward. Charlie charged with a vicious, snarling leap to the end of his lead, trying to get at the bear. He was frothing at the mouth, and his vicious barks and snarls were extraordinary. I kept up the barrage of flares, landing them on the ice close to the bear's paws. My aim had improved, and I was laying them where I wanted them to go. It worked. Under a deluge of burning flares at his feet, the bear backed away to the east in a wide circle. He was heading away from us in an almost northerly direction. Then he stopped, as if reluctant to give up. I fired four more flares, again close to his feet. That was too much for him—he left without his dinner. My hand shook so much as I laid down the flare gun that I almost dropped it. That had been a close call. Once again, I was concerned about the number of bears we were meeting. Again, I recalled Tony telling me: alone on foot was the most dangerous way for me to travel. No wonder he had urged me to take a dog team instead. I patted Charlie in thanks. I had been very close to letting him off his lead. If I had, he would still be out there in the storm, chasing the bear. I was glad it hadn't come to that. Charlie had settled down and seemed satisfied that the bear had left for good. I decided to trust his judgment and take shelter inside the tent from the wind, which by now had developed into a howling gale. I was so cold that all I could think of was the warmth of my sleeping bag.

Just as I was about to enter the tent, I looked back at Charlie. After eating, he normally curled up on the ice to sleep. Instead, he was watching me with a look that said, *What about me out in this cold?* Although I knew that he had slept on ice all his life, I felt an intense need for us to sit out the raging storm side by side. Perhaps, just this once, he could sleep in the tent vestibule where I kept my radio and boots. *Tomorrow*, I thought, *he can sleep in his normal place outside.* I walked back to him, unsnapped his lead, and said, "Okay, Charlie, you can sleep in the porch as a special treat." Without waiting to hear more, he raced into the tent and leaped onto my sleeping bag, which was already laid out for my cold, shivering body to slip into. With visions of warmth, I scrambled back to the tent, but the "Occupied" sign was up! Charlie had claimed it as his own. By now I was so cold that I had to get into that bag, but first of all Charlie had to move over. I pushed, pulled, begged, and loudly demanded, with absolutely no success. The more I pushed and pulled, the deeper he thrust his nose under his curled tail. It was clear that no amount of pushing, begging, and demanding was going to get this ninety-four-pound immovable object off my bag. I would just have to slide in alongside him and make do. As I eased into the narrow space beside him, I told him, "Charlie, when I warm up, you have to go." I wasn't comfortable, but at least I was warming up with the help of my sleeping bag and the warmth of Charlie's ample body. A half hour later I was reasonably warm. It was time to change tactics and reclaim my sleeping bag. I climbed out and prepared a comfortable area for him in the tent vestibule. Then I sat down on my bag and slid my feet underneath his body. He didn't like the two lumps wiggling under him. With a resigned sigh he sat up and sent me a reproachful look. In a flash I slid into the bag and spread out, taking up all the space. That did it. He gave up and ambled to the vestibule, curled up, and went to sleep.

Terry at base radioed the weather forecast. It wasn't good—more strong winds from the south. I worried about bears as the wind raced across the ice and slammed into the tent, because the noise of the wind and flapping tent were too loud to allow me to hear a bear. It was the first storm of our journey, and I wondered if Charlie could sense a bear in this awful racket. I hoped for good weather tomorrow and reached out to pat Charlie. My resolve to make him sleep outside the tent was slowly crumbling; it was a comfort to have him close.

Next morning, I awoke to the same howling winds. I didn't need to look outside to know that the storm was still with us. But in case there was a chance that we could travel, I had to check. I shook a still-sleeping Charlie, but his only response was to push his nose further under his bushy tail. His message was clear. He was not going to get up at that ungodly hour just to face a howling storm. He was smart! *Oh well,* I thought, *so much for company.*

I struggled with my still-frozen jacket, which I hadn't de-iced the night before. De-icing had become a nightly job. After several hours of skiing during the day, a thick layer of ice would form on my mask, down the front of my jacket, and yesterday even around the collar, making it difficult to turn my head and almost impossible to unzip my jacket. Each night I used my pocketknife to scrape ice off my mask and jacket zipper. But now the still-frozen zipper refused to cooperate, so I pulled on a hat and crawled out the door in my soft camp booties. When I stood up, the wind caught me with its full force. My unzipped jacket was thrown open and the wind poured into my sweater and inner clothing. I groped my way back to the tent door, trying desperately to protect my eyes, which were being blasted by driven snow. I dived through the door, practically falling over a still-sleeping Charlie. Relieved to escape the wind, I told him, "No traveling today, Charlie." There was no response. He had apparently figured it out, and had no intention of wasting precious energy checking on something he already knew. Even when I placed his pan of food beside him, he didn't so much as acknowledge it. Storms were nothing new to Charlie, and he instinctively knew how to survive them. My human reaction to the storm seemed lacking in comparison. I decided that since the storm was in control of our day's travel schedule, I should concentrate on our own tiny world inside the tent. I tried to not even think of my surroundings outside, especially bears. It was better to concentrate on preparing for the day ahead.

After I thawed ice for our day's water supply, I filled my thermoses, then heated water and added it to my bowl of granola and milk powder, along with a few peanut butter cups for a little variety. It tasted quite good, although I wouldn't recommend it as a gourmet delight. I followed up with a cup of hot chocolate. Charlie eventually woke up just long enough to eat his food, then promptly curled up for more sleep. As soon as I turned off the stove, the sound of the wind and flapping tent instantly replaced its noisy roar. It was almost noon by the clock, but real time was related directly to the storm. When it stopped, we could leave, and not before.

At five P.M. the wind still raged. The anemometer read a steady forty miles per hour, with gusts to forty-six. The temperature had warmed to minus 19 degrees. Discouraged, I wondered how long the storm would go on. Springtime storms from the south can be long and fierce. Carefully easing myself out the tent door, I crawled around the back of the tent. I scraped snow away from the walls and, using the shovel, pushed more snow up onto the snow skirt to prevent more snow from pushing against the tent walls. The fine-grained snow was impossible to pack. The wind drove the cold through my clothes and deep into my body. I hurried to check out the rest of the tie-downs and then scrambled back into the tent. I awoke many times during the night to the roar of the wind, and the high-pitched howl of even stronger gusts that blasted the tent, bending the walls inward. I thought of the miles we could have traveled by now. Whether I liked it or not, the weather was in control and I could do nothing but wait patiently for the chance to move onward.

The tent survived the night of brutal punishment, but at 9 next morning the storm still showed no sign of letting up. I decided to light the stove and make breakfast. After I set up the stove in the center of the floor, Charlie immediately moved in closer. He no doubt thought, *Oh good, she's making a meal just for me.* Of course, I shared my food, and when he begged for more peanut butter cups, of course I gave him mine. There seemed no limit to his capacity to figure out how to get me to share.

After breakfast I sat on my sleeping bag with my map spread across my knees, studying the route and miles ahead. Suddenly I was jolted by the sound of a loud crack outside the tent. The map flew in one direction and the sleeping bag in another as I jumped up, grabbing my rifle and unzipping the door. I saw nothing through the blowing snow. I waited, my nerves on edge, crouched in the doorway. *Surely a bear wouldn't make a sound that loud*, I thought. Charlie had jumped up as fast as I had, and crouched at my side. He too was alert and tense, but not as if he sensed a bear close by. *What in the world is going on?* Moments later, I had my answer. My whole body jumped in terror when once more an ear-splitting crack sounded above the noise of the storm. For an instant, just as I heard the sound, I saw a split slice through the ice five feet in front of the tent. Now it dawned on me what was happening. My worst fears were being realized. The storm was causing the ice to split apart and break up. Grabbing my jacket, hat, and goggles, I scrambled outside. I half crouched and crawled to a three-inch-wide split that began and ended out there somewhere in the blowing snow. I was relieved to see that it wasn't widening. There was a second, wider split six feet beyond the first one, but it wasn't widening either. I could see water only six inches down. Charlie and I were trapped in an area of thin ice, and the powerful winds were moving the ice pack in a grinding mass all around us. A clearly anxious Charlie was close at my side. Terrified that the ice might disintegrate and drop us into the ocean, I shoved him back into the tent. I dug my sled out from under two feet of snow, pulled it inside, and packed everything onto it as fast as I could. Charlie had moved to the back of the tent and sat alert and tense, watching. Next, I dug out his sled and food, and pulled the sled close to the door. I dressed and checked Charlie's harness. We were both ready to escape the tent at a moment's notice. My map showed that we were in an area called Penny Strait, where swift ocean currents thin the ice. All we could do was wait and hope the ice beneath us wouldn't break apart. The wind had become a screaming torrent. Our situation was worsening by the minute. I sat listening, my nerves stretched tight, when a loud, rumbling, thunder-like sound rolled from the far distance toward us, followed by the deafening sound of ice breaking up all around the tent. A startled Charlie leaped to his feet. We were in the midst of a major ice breakup caused by a powerful storm that could soon reduce our ice platform and the surrounding ice to mere ice cubes. We crouched close to the doorway, ready at the first sign of the ice giving way beneath us to escape the tent, which was by now convulsing in the wind like a wild thing. I prayed that the anchors and tent poles wouldn't give way and the ice beneath the tent would remain intact. Charlie was nervous and pressed even closer. I listened for any sound of the ice breaking beneath us. I had my hand on his collar, ready to get us both out of the tent in an instant. Now and then a screaming blast of wind hit us and shook the tent like an earthquake. But I was most worried about the ice, which I knew was being battered to pieces. This was not a good time to be sitting on an ice-covered ocean.

A half hour later, I was cramped and cold with inactivity. I rummaged in the food bag for some walnuts. I offered some to Charlie, but he didn't like them, so I got them all. The wind was as strong as ever, but the ice was less noisy now. Hoping that the emergency was over, I began setting up things for the night. Suddenly a series of three or four rifle-like cracks sent me, with a pounding heart, to the doorway to see what was going on outside. Two new cracks had knifed their way north to south through the ice. The nearest, a pencil-thin line, was only two feet from the side of the tent. Crouching in the wind, trying to protect myself from the blowing snow that felt like sand blasting my exposed skin, I heard more rifle-like sounds in the distance as the ice continued to break apart in the storm. Quickly returning to the shelter of the tent to escape the wind, I tried to decide what we should do. Poor Charlie was a nervous and unhappy fellow. The sound of breaking ice had scared him too. I put my arm around him and hoped that he couldn't sense my own worry. My nerves were shattering just like the ice around us, and our situation was close to overwhelming. *Will the ice beneath the tent break and drop us into the ocean?* Although I was desperate to leave this awful place with its wind and breaking ice, it was impossible to leave while the storm raged and visibility was reduced to a few feet. All we could do was remain sheltered and as warm as possible, and be ready for whatever happened. After all, I reasoned, the storm wouldn't last forever.

I left both sleds fully packed. I finished the fluid from my thermoses and ate a few cashews that didn't require unpacking. I could reach Charlie's food, so I fed him. All that we could do now was try to get some sleep and wait. But first, unable to resist the urge to check for more ice cracks, I donned my jacket and hat and once more faced the elements. The closest crack in the front of the tent had widened to six or seven inches, but the second one had closed up. The pencil line that had split only two feet from the side of the tent was almost a foot across, and the rest were either closed or a little wider than before. All signs showed that the ice was still moving. I decided to sleep in all of my clothes, even my boots, to be ready for instant flight. My greatest fear was that if the ice split beneath us, we would have to abandon the tent in a hurry. I really needed to get some sleep, but my heart just wasn't in it. I dozed off, but kept waking up—listening for the dreaded sound of breaking ice amid the howl of the wind.

About midnight the wind began to lessen. The high-pitched howl was gone and the tent walls were quieter. My prayers were being answered. The storm was at long last moving on. At two A.M. I took a hopeful look out the door. The wind was blowing at half its former strength, but visibility was still too low through the swirling snow for me to get any real information. I would have to get a clear look at the ice ahead before we set off, to avoid the risk of falling through any unseen openings. Our world was still only a few feet wide. I returned to a tense, restless doze. Charlie slept close at my side. He appeared to relax when he could actually touch me. It seemed to give him reassurance. No doubt he longed to get away from this dangerous place as much as I did.

Toward morning the wind continued to slacken, but it wasn't until six A.M. that I could see far enough ahead to travel. The ice fog that had developed earlier was gone, and visibility had increased to about a quarter of a mile. A chaotic jumble of broken ice awaited us outside. After eating a quick bite—a handful of crackers and walnuts for me, and dog food for Charlie—I packed up and we headed out to meet the challenge. The minus 15 degrees was warmer than the last few days. Did that mean that another storm was on the way? The wind, although now slight, was still from the south, which meant the weather was unsettled enough to bring a storm. The first thing I did was look for splits and gaps in the ice. Our real estate had shrunk down to an ice island only about thirty feet across, and our situation was desperate. We had to escape before another storm turned the already fragile area into a certain death trap.

Charlie's intense dislike of water made him nervous, and he stood as close to me and as far from the edge of the ice as he could manage. This made a marked contrast to his confidence when facing a polar bear. The gap separating our floating ice island from our course ahead was only a foot across. Charlie hesitated, but when I stepped across, pulling both sleds behind me, he quickly followed. I looked down at the inky blackness of the water and shuddered, thinking of what it would be like to fall in. The sudden cold shock would be paralyzing and possibly fatal, so I could understand Charlie's concern. A few minutes later we stood on the edge of a chaotic jumble of broken ice floating amid wide areas of open, frigid water. I was surprised at the thinness of the ice pack, only a few inches thick in places and only two feet thick in others. It was a contrast to the thicker ice we had been traveling over the last few days, which explained why it had fractured under the stress of the storm. With my ski pole, I pushed pieces of ice together to form a bridge between the two closest ice pans. I piled more ice on top to make it thicker. Hoping that the bridge was strong enough, I linked Charlie's sled to the back of mine and cautiously pulled them across. The bridge held. At low temperatures chunks of ice adhere easily to each other, and I could see that if I piled enough ice to form a bridge at least a foot thick, it would hold my weight and that of the sled as long as I wore skis to spread out my weight. I had Charlie on a long lead and urged him to follow me. At first, he stared down at the water and refused to move. After I gently pulled on his lead and called to him, he made it safely across. Keeping him on a separate lead in case he fell into the water gave me the means to pull him to safety if necessary. I anxiously looked ahead, trying to see the safest way forward. Leaning lightly against my leg, Charlie waited for me to decide on our route ahead. He had developed this habit of contact when we were around open water or he was unsure of my next move. In return, I had learned to give him definite physical signals to indicate the plan ahead. It was a precious gift to be trusted by a dog who had never learned trust or known real human kindness.

All at once the ice began to move again, cracking and grinding in all directions. Terrified, I watched the gap in front of me slowly close to only inches across. The tides and swift currents were moving even the fractured area beneath our feet. Quickly taking advantage of the now-narrow split, we stepped across. The next gap a few yards away was wider and slowly opening. I grabbed Charlie, urging him to hurry as we scrambled over that one too. But then there was a sharp boom and a crack raced through the ice just inches in front of my ski tips. My mouth went dry with fear. We had to get away, and as fast as possible. We crossed the new split only to reach the edge of a gap almost three feet across. Afraid that it would suddenly widen, I quickly attached a long rope to Charlie's sled so that he could jump across without his sled pulling him backward. His head tilted with uncertainty as he watched me approach the gap. I was able to use my skis as a bridge, although they bent alarmingly in the middle. They reached across the gap and I stepped across, pulling my sled over after me. Poor Charlie had reached his limit. A few inches were all right, but this? I leaned toward him with my hand outstretched, calling his name and trying to sound calm and confident. After a few moments of staring down at the water, he jumped. His powerful body sailed over easily and gracefully. All I had to do was pull his sled over. I patted him and praised him to show how impressed I was. Looking pleased with himself, he responded to my big hug with a lick across my face that I interpreted as a kiss.

The ice fog had disappeared, making it easier to look ahead for the safest route. I stopped to listen. The ice was silent. Perhaps we had heard its last convulsion. We crossed many more splits and gaps, the widest no more than three feet across. Charlie was doing fine. My pulling his sled made it easier and safer for him to jump across the gaps. He walked at my side, trusting me completely. Now, as we wound our way across and around the fractured ice, he never hesitated, sometimes even jumping ahead of me. Ahead were more gaps wide enough to require bridges. With increasing confidence in my bridge building, I continued onward. Charlie was reluctant to cross the fragile structures, but they were all we had to reach the thicker ice. Finally, each time he agreed, but he wanted to walk close at my side. The bridges were too narrow for that, so I hitched him to the last sled so he could follow close behind. I had depended on Charlie to warn and protect me from polar bears; now it was his turn to depend on me to get us safely out of our predicament.

After a long and incredibly hard fifteen-hour day, we eventually reached ice that was at least a foot or two thick. It was a relief beyond description to at last stand on something reasonably solid. Charlie apparently thought so too. He quickly relaxed and returned to his usual confident self. I was relieved that we were both alive and had escaped the watery depths. I untied Charlie's sled from mine and attached it to his harness, and we continued on. We didn't even stop to eat or drink. All I wanted was to put more distance between us and the hellish jumble of ice we had left behind.

The mind-numbing fear of polar bears never let go. By now I was dealing with only one day at a time—or, whenever I knew that a bear was close by or we crossed fairly fresh tracks, one hour at a time. But also by now, I was confident that Charlie would take care of any bears we would meet.

An hour after clearing the thin and broken ice area, I wearily stopped for our first break. First I fed Charlie, but he surprised me by ignoring his food and instead looked to share mine. I made a point of ignoring his begging. I moved his pan to sit right under his nose. I told him in a tone that I hoped sounded authoritative, "Eat your own food!" Still, he ignored his food and continued to beg for mine. Charlie's ability to beg could not be taken lightly. He appeared determined to have his way. Now it turned into a battle of wills. Turning my back on him, I continued to eat and drink. At first he tried to circle to face me, but I silently turned away. After several minutes and with an attitude of deep resignation, he consented to eat his food while sending frequent, hopeful glances in my direction. I was mildly surprised that I had achieved a small victory. I fussed over him to show that his efforts were well appreciated. He ignored my fussing as if to punish me for my inconsiderate ways, but when I produced three crackers and two peanut butter cups, his attitude radiated forgiveness. All was well between us once more.

Although it was definitely time to stop and make camp for a well-earned rest, I dared not do so just then. While we were eating, I had heard long-drawn-out groans interspersed with high-pitched screeches rising from beneath our feet, a sure sign that even though we had left the broken, unstable ice behind us, the ice was still moving with the fast-flowing ocean currents that flowed past the diminutive Cheyne Islands that lay ahead. After studying my map, I decided to ski on until I was certain that we could camp on stable ice. The relentless struggle had left my body beyond tired. Numb with fatigue, my mind had reached the stage of forcing one ski ahead of the other, insensitive to anything but the desperate need to keep going. Charlie, his steps not as brisk as usual, was doing an incredible job of staying close to my side, keeping pace. Although he was a true champion without complaint, I felt guilty about asking him travel an unreasonably long day. But I was sure that if he could have spoken, he would have agreed that we had to avoid repeating the many hours we had just spent struggling to avoid plunging through thin, broken ice into the watery abyss below. It was hard to believe that only two weeks ago this faithful dog didn't even have a name.

It wasn't long before we crossed a fresh set of bear tracks. Instantly Charlie, with his nose pressed to the ice, plunged off in determined pursuit. The tracks headed north along the direction we were traveling. I had no desire to catch up with a bear. Pulling back on Charlie's leash, I yelled, "Stop!" Even though he stopped, his momentum caused his sled to slide past me, careening sideways off a two-foot mound of ice, and dart across my ski tips. It had the effect of suddenly slamming the brakes on my skis, pitching me forward over my ski tips. I landed on my face in a tangle of ski poles and skis. I looked up, and there was Charlie calmly gazing back at me. His puzzled expression clearly said, *What on earth are you doing now?* It was not a happy moment. Having my face rammed into the ice was no fun, and I could feel the anger rising. Then I remembered how guilty I had felt the other day when I became angry with Charlie over what was really only a minor offense. With a large measure of self-control, I kept a firm grip on my feelings while I attempted to untangle my body, skis, and poles. *After all,* I reminded myself, *it's the most natural thing in the world for Charlie to want to chase polar bears.* I just wished he wouldn't do it while pulling his sled. He appeared completely unaware that he had been the cause of the commotion and lay comfortably on the ice resting, while I got myself upright and pointed in the right direction again.

Ahead, I noticed patches of unusually dark gray ice at least fifty feet across that signaled the newly formed heavily salt-laden ice that are called nilas. The darker the gray, the more salt it contains and the more likely a skier will break through. Two hours later, after skirting the thinner ice, a tired Charlie lay down every time I stopped to scout the way ahead. His message was clear. *When do we camp?* I hated to tell him to keep going, and it must have been puzzling to him to try to figure out why we couldn't stop. My sled, which had become an extension of my body, now seemed many times heavier as we continued onward in search of a safe place to camp.

At seven P.M. we at last reached stable ice and stopped. It was pure relief to drop my sled-pulling harness and step out of my skis. Even before I put the tent up Charlie had curled up on the ice and fallen asleep, clearly thankful to at last end a long, hard day. After setting up camp I woke Charlie, and to his delight, ushered him into the tent vestibule with his pan of food, which he hastily munched before returning to a sound sleep. Later the south wind increased to fifteen miles per hour, kicking snow high off the ice. A deep chill settled over us as the fading sun slowly sank below the horizon without really setting, lighting the nights of the twenty-four-hour days that were now following us to the Pole. Too tired to cook or even melt ice for water, I wearily climbed into my sleeping bag to end an impossibly, long grueling day and I joined Charlie in deep sleep.

Hard going at a pressure ridge

Happy to end a long hard day

Mother with Cubs

Chapter Seven —
A Showdown for Survival

Sometime after midnight I awoke to a howling windstorm that shook the tent. Charlie was curled up, still asleep, undisturbed by the fury unleashed on our tiny home. Six hours later the storm still showed no signs of letting up, so I lit my stove to melt ice for breakfast. At the sound of the noisy stove Charlie woke up, stretched, and looked over my shoulder to see what I was taking out of the food bag. He saw crackers and leaned over to help himself. "No, Charlie!" I said. He hesitated, then turned to his dog food, keeping an eye on me to see what he might steal or beg. After eating half his food, he stood, looking sleepy, watching me pour water onto my granola. Then, deciding that I was going to keep it all for myself, he turned around, curled up, and went back to sleep.

Now almost two weeks into the expedition, I had become lazy and often mixed granola, rice, milk powder, and even a few crackers together for a meal. Though monotonous, it was filling and served its purpose. I was not overly concerned about food on expeditions as long as it gave me the sustenance and energy to continue day after day, and would normally eat without mental comment.

Still, as I looked at the lukewarm mess in my bowl, I told myself I should really make an attempt to at least eat things separately. But then, idly pondering the problem further, I decided it made some sense to eat one-dish meals. The whole meal was over and done with much faster and with less fiddling around. Having rationalized my lazy cooking habits, I finished the last spoonful and sat back on my sleeping bag to plan the day. There wasn't much to plan. Charlie and I couldn't go anywhere in the storm. I tried waking Charlie to urge him closer to me for company. Perhaps I could tell him of my thoughts and plans. Even a one-way conversation would have been better than none. There was no response, so I gave up and decided that I would have to entertain myself since my tent-mate seemed interested only in sleeping.

At noon I heated water for another uninspiring meal, followed by hot chocolate. As I filled my thermoses, I noticed lengthening gaps of silence between the gusts of wind that howled around the tent. The storm was passing, and I thought it could be time to pack up in case we could leave soon. But when I looked out, all I could see was snow being picked up off the ice and rearranged in ridges around the tent. By three o'clock the wind had gone on its way and Charlie and I were bathed in a welcome silence, broken only by an occasional low groan or high-pitched whine from deep within the ice pack beneath the tent. Visibility was reduced to no more than three or four feet. The still air was a blanket of tiny snowflakes that floated lazily down to land quietly on the ice. Still concerned over the possibility of stumbling into open water or crossing thin ice too weak to support our weight, I dared not start out without being able to see at least a few yards ahead. By seven that night the snow had stopped and the air was thick with ice fog. The temperature had risen to 9 degrees. I walked away from the tent, trying to decide if we should break camp and head out. At fifteen feet away, I looked back and could barely see the tent through the blanket of white that hung like a thick curtain around me.

Back in the tent, I studied my map. Our present position was close to the northern tip of Bathurst Island, where I could turn northwest. I remembered the gray patches of thin new ice that we had woven our way through yesterday. There were more ahead of us along our route, and they would be invisible in the whiteness that now reduced our world to a few square feet. Until I could see those patches, we couldn't travel safely. I grew more frustrated by the hour. Sitting there felt worse than struggling through a fifteen-hour day. I was hoping the wind would move around to the north. A northerly wind would bring back good weather and clear visibility. Never again would I complain about the cold north wind, I resolved. I kept checking outside, trying to detect even the faintest wind shift to the north. The nightly radio call to Terry wasn't reassuring. "You might get more wind up there yet." Heeding her warning, I checked the tent tie-downs and made sure that everything was securely anchored.

I woke Charlie, who looked at his food, pushed it around in his pan, and then sleepily lay down again. When I poured warm water into his pan, his reaction was total disinterest. After a few minutes I poured it out before it froze. That seemed to trigger an instinct in Charlie. He suddenly got to his feet, walked to the end of his lead, began digging a shallow hole in the ice, and then ate the fine pieces of ice he dug up. Returning to the tent vestibule, he dug another shallow hole in the ice and lay in it. I knew Charlie had eaten ice all his life and wasn't used to someone offering him pans of warm water. But I had noticed before leaving base camp that his urine, and that of other dogs in the village, was dark, almost orange yellow, indicating they weren't getting enough liquid. To ensure that Charlie would be properly hydrated and to protect his kidneys, I had loaded extra fuel onto my sled so that I could melt ice for Charlie. At the beginning of the expedition, he would just look at the water rather than drink it, and it quickly froze in the pan. He had gradually accepted more water each day during the journey, but still preferred ice. After the eighth day his urine was a lighter color, so I knew the extra trouble of melting ice, and figuring out how to get him to drink it before it froze, was paying off.

Around two A.M. the sound of the tent flapping in the wind stirred me from a sound sleep. By four o'clock we were engulfed in another howling gale. When I stepped out of the tent to check that my sled was solidly anchored, the wind sent me reeling. I regained my balance and peered into the gray gloom, but saw that visibility was still only a few feet, making it impossible to watch for bears or open water. I scrambled back into the shelter of the tent. This was the thirteenth day of the expedition, and I was exasperated and angry over the constant weather delays.

Then, in the midst of my frustration, a glimmer of reason took hold and grew. I looked at Charlie sleeping the storm away. He had taken control by simply accepting the storm and sleeping through it. He would be rested and ready to go when the time came. The Arctic classroom and Charlie were teaching me yet another lesson. Taking a hint from his example, I decided to eat breakfast. As I examined the mix of granola, butter, milk powder, coconut, and a few crackers and peanut butter cups I had thrown into my bowl, I once again felt its shortcomings. To make time pass more quickly, I decided to be more creative. I poured my mix into Charlie's pan as I inquired, "Would you like this, Charlie?" In an instant he was awake, and after taking a brief moment to understand his good fortune, he consumed the lot in a few gulps, then sat expectantly waiting for more. It was time to serve breakfast for two. The main course would be granola, milk powder, and butter, with a light sprinkling of coconut flakes. For the first time I carefully measured all ingredients. This would be followed by two cups of hot chocolate made with hot water instead of the usual fuel-conserving lukewarm version. Instead of plain crackers for Charlie, I spread a thick coating of butter on each one, much to his delight. His beloved peanut butter cups followed. Then—I'm sure to his amazement—I invited him to sit on the other half of my sleeping bag while I served breakfast. He spread his ample body in total comfort to take full advantage of my offer, probably hardly believing the treasure that I placed before him. A small piece of toilet paper made an excellent table napkin for me. Charlie didn't need one. Background music for an intimate breakfast for two was supplied by the wind as it alternately whistled and roared around the shaking tent. Time flew by as I mixed and poured. If time passed more quickly, the storm did not. The morning was almost gone, but the wind was still thrashing the tent, its monotonous roar deadening my listening senses.

Charlie's unconcerned manner was a good example and I decided to copy him and catch up on my sleep. After much shoving and pushing, I moved Charlie over and slid into my sleeping bag. With a disappointed grunt he ambled off to the vestibule and curled up for sleep. But it wasn't long before he woke me when he sprawled down at my side and lay his head over my chest. I informed him, "You might be comfortable, but I am not!" We had to agree to a new arrangement. I pushed him off me and sat up. Apparently, all was not to his liking, and he pressed in closer to my side. To compromise, I emptied my clothing bag and spread a few spare clothes alongside my sleeping bag. Now Charlie was satisfied. He quickly took advantage of the new arrangement and fell asleep spread out on the makeshift bed alongside me while I, now that I had enough room in my sleeping bag, did the same.

I must have slept for no more than an hour when I was suddenly awakened by the sounds of ice creaking and popping beneath the tent. It's common when camped on an ice-covered ocean to hear the movement of ice under tension, especially while sleeping, when one's head is closer to the ice. But these sounds were louder than normal. I sat up, startled by the percussion of cracks, creaks, and booms that echoed through the ice. Thinking, *Surely not another ice breakup,* I scrambled on all fours to the doorway and looked out, dreading what I might see. The ice looked solid and the wind had died. To make sure, I circled the tent and saw no signs that the ice was splitting. With an immense sense of relief, I slid back through the tent door. In my haste to exit the tent I had disturbed Charlie, who now sat looking sleepy and disgruntled at such a rude awakening. I patted him my apologies and returned to my sleeping bag. The orchestra of sounds continued, but I decided that it was just another day of living on an ocean ice pack that was always in motion to some extent.

By midmorning the wind was quiet, and although an ice fog thickened the air, visibility had improved enough to allow us to leave. Charlie was in a playful mood and ready to go. He rolled on the ice, scratching his back. I packed in a record half hour, happy to be on our way again. When I hitched him to his almost empty sled, he started to leave without me. I admired his enthusiasm, but I called him back. After all, I was supposed to be the leader on this expedition. Fastening my harness to my sled, we left at a fast pace in an effort to make up for lost time.

Charlie made it known that he was impatient to pick up speed and wanted to lead me. For the first mile I let him, but after constantly correcting his version of navigation, which was determined by his spirited need to follow the polar bear tracks that we crossed, I decided that our original arrangement worked best for us both. I called him back to my side. At first he feigned deafness, but finally conceded defeat, though without good grace. His outrage at having to give up the lead made clear his disappointment at having to ignore those tracks and tempting bear scent. We had traveled together for so long now that I could easily read his thoughts, as I'm sure he could read mine.

A mile later we ran into trouble. The wind had packed the snow into rock-hard ridges, ranging from a few inches to two feet high, with troughs of deep soft snow in between. It was very different from the smooth blanket of wind-packed snow that had covered the ice before the storm. With my skis strapped to my sled, I started to walk, but found myself sinking up to my knees in the soft snow between the ridges. Dragging my sled behind me, it felt as if I was pulling through glue. I floundered through each trough, climbing over the ridges, then floundered again on the other side. Charlie was pawing his way through the glue-like snow. In the worst troughs only his upper back and head showed above the surface. We were both using a lot of energy to force our way through, and Charlie was using even more energy to just stay upright. After an hour of hard work, we had covered only about a mile and the wind gusts had pushed us away to the right. I was still determined to continue onward to make a few miles, even when a particularly vicious gust knocked us both sideways, almost dumping me on top of Charlie.

An hour later the ever-strengthening wind forced a halt. I'm sure that Charlie, now plastered with snow, agreed. It was time to give up the fight and make camp. My main concern now was to erect the tent without the nylon fabric ripping or bending a pole. Finally, after I had done much scrambling on all fours and screwed ice screws into the rock-hard ice with fingers that not only grew colder by the minute, but also still throbbed from their bout with frostbite, the tent was up. While the cold deepened, my next task was to get into the tent to warm up out of the wind before taking essential equipment out of my sled. I was halfway through the doorway when a determined Charlie, who apparently had the same idea, pushed past me. Mildly annoyed, I first informed him that he needed lessons in good manners. But then I thought, *Never mind, he needs to warm up too.* It turned out that his goal was to claim the back half of the tent and wait for the sleeping bag to arrive. Then, in keeping with his latest custom, he stretched out on the bag in comfort, waiting for his dinner. By now I had resigned myself to trusting that he would be able to sense any approaching bears even when he was inside the tent. At least I hoped so!

At four o'clock the wind was down to no more than a breeze. I dressed and packed, determined to set a fast pace and ski as many miles as possible before stopping for the night. My spirits were high. Perhaps the wind had at last spent itself and good weather had returned. With Charlie watching my progress, I was gathering items to load on my sled when suddenly there was a loud crunch in the ice outside the tent.

We both knew what it was: a bear! Charlie, with a lion-like deafening roar, dashed outside to the end of his lead. With a pounding heart, I grabbed the rifle and scrambled out the door to be confronted by a female bear standing a short distance away, her black eyes fixed on us, no doubt surprised at Charlie's sudden aggressive appearance. Taken aback, she took a few quick steps backward while Charlie, in a snarling rage, leaped at her again and again. I jerked the flare gun from my pocket and quickly fired a row of flares at her feet. But it was Charlie and his ferocious act that held her attention. With her eyes riveted on him she took several quick steps backward, then moved to our left to stay well out of range of Charlie's frenzied leaps. The bear looked thin, which meant that she was probably desperate to find food, and apparently I was on her menu. Changing direction, she swung to our right, and although staying out of Charlie's reach, she wasn't leaving. As my pounding heart and fear reached new heights, I continued firing flares at her feet while Charlie's lunges and snarls kept her back. It began to look like a standoff. I checked my flare ammunition. I always kept two pockets full of shells. My rifle was loaded, and I had more rifle shells at the ready in a row of loops sewn across the front of my jacket. The bear swept to the left again, then surprised me by turning and, without changing stride, walking to some scattered low chunks of ice about two hundred feet farther to the left. To my amazement two small bundles of white fur emerged from their hiding place and trotted side by side to their mother. She led them a few more yards away to a flat area and lay down with her belly exposed to allow her cubs to feed. For a moment I wondered if I was seeing things, and even forgot my pounding heart. It was a beautiful sight to see her attending to her motherly duties, although it seemed odd that she would feed her cubs in full view of Charlie and me. It could only mean that—now that she was some distance away, and Charlie had quieted down as soon as she retreated—she considered us nonthreatening. I assumed that she had been curious to investigate the unfamiliar blue tent she found along her path. I looked down and saw her paw prints etched into the snow only six feet directly in front of the tent doorway. She had been so close!

Now, only two hundred feet away, she appeared to ignore us—although because of her concern about Charlie, I'm sure she must have kept one eye on him. I wasn't convinced that she would leave, so I decided to strengthen my defenses. I grabbed my jacket and zipped it, then reached for my hat and liner gloves, since my large mitts were too clumsy to use with the flare gun and rifle. I grabbed another three boxes of flares and laid them with a new box of rifle ammunition on top of my sled, then stood ready with my flare gun and rifle fully loaded, while Charlie, his body rigid and poised for action and his eyes riveted on the bear, made no sound. Total silence pressed in from all sides. A long, tense twenty minutes later, the bear rose to her feet, nuzzled her cubs, and led them away through an area of broken ice with her nose held low, in a hunting mood, looking for seal breathing holes. For the moment at least, we were safe. With the cubs following right on her heels, the bear swung in a wide roaming circle as she slowly worked her way through the scattered blocks of ice. Every so often she raised her nose in the air, as if trying to catch the scent of a seal. She continued her close inspection until she arrived back at the area where she had fed her cubs. They milled about for a few minutes. Then, leaving her cubs behind some low mounds off to the side, she turned in our direction once more. She approached us with the same slow, plodding walk she had used while hunting and stopped a hundred feet away. Charlie began to growl and strain at the end of his lead. After failing to find a seal breathing hole, had the bear decided that I might be an easier target? Her determination not to leave had me worried. I fired more flares and, with my right hand on Charlie's collar, I prepared to press the release catch if the bear showed any signs of a charge. I felt Charlie's powerful neck muscles vibrate with his furious growling. No more than a hundred feet away, the bear's black beady eyes watched us as she circled. Every fiber of my body waited for the first sign of a charge. The air was electric. Then, ever so slowly, she stepped back, swinging her head from side to side with her nose held high to catch our scent. I stared back at her, not daring to move in case she interpreted any movement as flight. She moved with silent, flowing strides to our right and began circling the still-standing tent. I turned to face her as she circled, keeping my hand on Charlie's collar.

Now I was faced with a dilemma. Should I fire my rifle and shoot her, hoping that a single shot would kill her? I knew that a wounded bear would turn into an instant killing machine. And what fate would her cubs face if I shot their mother? Or should I let Charlie go to deal with the bear as he had earlier on? He had returned unscathed after the last chase, but would he be so lucky now? I didn't want to risk Charlie unless it was absolutely necessary. So far, Charlie's wild, vicious, snarling lunges had held her back. He repeatedly charged at her with teeth bared, frothing at the mouth, with eardrum-piercing snarls and growls. Wary of him, she kept her distance and continued to circle. Passing minutes seemed years long. My nerves were taut as I stood ready to either fire my rifle or release Charlie.

Two hours passed in slow motion. Now my nerves had passed the screaming stage; they were numb. At every moment I faced the same terrible dilemma. Should I shoot and get it over with, or should I wait? I felt cold, especially my thinly clad hands against the steel of my rifle, but I dared not take my eyes off her to reach for more clothes or gloves. Exhaustion set in from the grinding need for absolute concentration. As Charlie and I continued to circle to keep our eyes on the bear, he kept up a continuous barrage of growls. After what seemed a lifetime, she stopped as if unsure whether to continue her circling or leave. I waited, not moving, ready to let Charlie off his lead if she charged. Time stood still and the surrounding world disappeared, leaving the two of us in a showdown for survival. After a few more anxious minutes she turned, stopped once to look back, then walked in the direction of her cubs as they scampered across the ice to meet her in a joyful reunion. Nuzzling each one for a brief moment, she led them away across their icy world in a northerly direction with her head down, hunting seals as before. She had stalked us for four of the longest hours of my life.

Ignoring the cold, I stood for many long minutes watching her leave, hoping that this time she was gone for good. Charlie was relaxed, as if he sensed it was over. But I was skeptical. I couldn't unwind until I was sure she wouldn't return. It was a half hour before I dared to allow myself to believe that she had really left. With Charlie at the forefront, we had won the right to survive. Overcome, I sank to my sled. I looked up to see Charlie watching me. A look of understanding passed between us. Once more he had done his job well. He had proved again that he would sacrifice his life to save mine. I patted him a heartfelt thanks and scratched his back. He wriggled with pleasure. It seemed an inadequate reward, but a good back scratch was always welcome.

It was so late that I decided to camp, eat, sleep, and get an early start in the morning. We had lost several hours of good traveling, but time to relax and let my overtaxed nerves recover would be welcome.

Radioing base camp

A little rest after another long day

In the Arctic, on a clear day sunlight is reflected off an ice-covered ocean causing the sky to show as light blue, rather than the deeper blue of skies occurring at lower latitudes.

A watery void to avoid

Chapter Eight —
Escaping the Void

At midnight the wind had at last turned to the north. It was a picturesque, clear morning so I decided to break camp. The days and nights had by now become one, with twenty-four hours of daylight. We could travel any time, day or night, to allow us to catch up for the time we had lost due to storms and bear encounters. I'd had enough of stormy Arctic weather and didn't want to chance another delay.

I had already hitched Charlie to his sled, which was now almost empty. As soon as I began loading my sled he was on his feet, ready for an early start. All around my tent site and ahead for a quarter mile there were low mounds of rough ice, but I was encouraged by seeing improved ice ahead. I took in the view that had been invisible in the storm. The one-hundred-foot-high cliffs to my left on Bathurst were covered with long, gleaming tongues of ice that reached all the way down to sea level. Ahead I saw a wide, blank area of sea ice, a shadowless white in the midnight light. I stared ahead, hoping we wouldn't encounter more areas of treacherous thin ice like those we had cautiously traveled across yesterday.

At first the ice looked white and thick. So far, no problems. But as I followed the coastline one mile to Cape Kitson, I noticed that the ice was becoming increasingly thin, slightly mushy, and colored gray where the ice had newly formed. I stayed close to the coast as I rounded the cape, looking for an escape to the safety of the land. I found a wide gully that led to the top of a three-hundred-foot plateau. From there I could cut across the corner of the island and find safer ice on the northern coast. After a long uphill haul, we stood on top of the plateau and I looked across a breathtaking view. The elongated, sprawling Loney Island, named for an early Arctic explorer, was three miles north of us, separated from Bathurst by ice-covered Water Sound. It was almost three A.M. and the sun rose from just below the horizon, pushing a wave of golden light across the ice and land that was empty of anything human. The wind had left and nothing moved. There was only a deep penetrating silence. This Arctic wasteland was indifferent to our presence. It had existed for centuries and would continue to exist long after our brief passing.

I turned away from my thoughts and walked northwest across the plateau, hoping to find an easy route down the cliffs of the as-yet-unseen north coast. The plateau was a tortured place, battered by winds that had plastered the driven snow into rock-hard slabs. Intermittent patches of rock-hugging lichen survived the brutal punishment dished out year after year. Areas of brown, sharp-edged rocks split into abrasive gravel poked through the snow and ice. When I could find no way around the rocks, they acted as brakes when my sled runners scraped across them.

Finally, we stood above the high cliffs of the northern coastline. The cliffs themselves were too steep and icy, but a little farther west there was a sloping ramp that descended about four hundred yards down to the sea ice just before a frozen river mouth. Although steep, it looked to be the only way down. I unhitched Charlie from his sled. He was no dog to miss an opportunity for play. Freed from his sled he bounded around in circles, daring me to chase him. Worried about the descent, I was not really in the mood for play—but how could I refuse? I lunged, trying to grab a handful of fur, but he sped up at exactly the right moment to avoid my outstretched hand. Then, emboldened to try new tactics, he crouched down, ready to pounce on me as I dashed by. I was no match for him and finally, out of breath, I told him, "We must get going, Charlie." He ignored me as if I had never spoken and nonchalantly wandered over to examine a nearby rock. His detailed inspection over, he then lifted his leg to relieve himself. It was clear that he considered the game of chase more important and thought such delaying tactics might persuade me to agree. He moved on to inspect another rock. This was too much! In a louder and more forceful tone, I told him that playtime was over and we had to get going now! He hesitated a moment as if contemplating his next move, then gave up and stood waiting for me. His dejected look clearly informed me that I was suffering from a serious lack of good judgment. I felt guilty at stopping his play, but I explained to him, "We need to get down that steep slope all in one piece."

Tying Charlie's sled to mine, I turned them both around and eased them down the slope in front of me, leaning back, using my body weight as a brake. After a few anxious out-of-control slides, I finally managed to get Charlie and me, and both sleds, safely down to the coast. Once on the sea ice I stopped for a quick snack before moving on. Charlie shared in all except the walnuts. My raw, frostbitten hands were throbbing from holding tightly to the sled ropes during our descent down the icy slope. They were improving, but still bled and split easily. I checked Charlie's paws to make sure he hadn't suffered any cuts in the sharp gravel, but as usual they were in excellent shape. Although I carried dog booties on my sled in case he needed them, his paws never suffered any problems over the entire journey.

The surface ahead was a mass of hard-packed snow swirls and ridges, some as high as two feet, a result of the wind funneled at high speed between Loney Island and the northern cliffs of Bathurst during the last storm. I decided to walk without skis because it was easier to move around the ridges, which were almost circular in places. Ahead lay Carey Harbor, a narrow, almost landlocked area of ice one mile wide and five miles long, hemmed in on each side by four-hundred-foot-high cliffs. A sinister stillness draped the landscape. Nothing moved in the incredibly deep silence. I was reminded not only of how isolated and far away from any human habitation we were, but that as we traveled north to the Pole, we would become even more isolated. When I was hemmed in by high cliffs, the sense of extreme isolation and even loneliness bore down on my shoulders like a lead weight. I marveled that these most inhospitable of all places were named, even though no one had ever lived there and humans rarely even visited. I hurried over the packed, ridged snow, trying not to notice the high intimidating cliffs, the silence, and the fact that Charlie and I were the only living things there. But this was nothing compared to what I would soon see.

Reaching the far end of the frozen harbor, we climbed a stretch of land that rose gently two hundred feet over the course of a mile and a half, then sloped down to a two-and-a-half-mile narrow fjord flanked on both sides by cliffs that rose almost straight up for five hundred feet, throwing the full length of the fjord into deep ominous shadow. My spirits sank. The sense of extreme isolation weighed me down. I instinctively reached for Charlie. I stroked his ears as he pressed into me. Thankful to have him at my side, I looked with dread at the shadowed ribbon of ice locked between high, lifeless cliffs. The fjord curved slightly just enough to hide the outlet from where we stood. We would be hemmed in. All I could think of was, *What will happen if we meet a bear here? We'll be trapped*. I dreaded going down into the shadowed void. There was only one thing I could do: set a course right down the middle, ski as fast as possible, and hope we wouldn't meet company. Already we had covered twenty-two miles since starting out after midnight, in spite of the much slower pace of overland travel. Now it was one in the afternoon and my goal was to reach Allard Island, thirteen miles away.

Soon Charlie, who had been calmly walking at my side, apparently not sharing my fear, pulled hard a few yards to the right. I looked in horror at fresh bear tracks that led right down the fjord ahead. The fear of being trapped in this awful place made my heart skip a few beats. I could only hope the bear was traveling far ahead of us and wouldn't detect our scent. Dread of meeting this or any bear made my skis slide across the ice faster than ever. My one thought was to escape this place.

Charlie had no such worries. With nose pressed to the tracks, he strode ahead. I'm sure he was happy that at last he could have his way and follow bear tracks without me pulling him away and telling him, *"No."* Perhaps he even hoped there might be a good bear chase at the end. The ice, tinted green, was mostly free of snow and made for fast skiing. Willing my skis to go faster, I searched ahead to see the outlet. After an hour, there it was in the distance, beyond which was light, space, and escape from the feeling of being trapped and blocked in by high cliffs and deep shadows. Breaking out of the fjord, I skied ahead into Craft Sound, free from the fjord and the awful darkness of my dread. The bear tracks branched away to the east and away from our route. I turned west, but Charlie tugged his lead to turn east to follow the bear's tracks. I pulled on his lead to follow me. His answer was to sit and express his outrage with short sharp barks of protest. "Come on, Charlie," I urged. With abject misery he looked at me as if thinking, *Is she really giving up the chance of a bear chase?* He finally consented to follow, but was in an unforgiving mood. It was some time before he let the incident pass and returned to his usual good-natured self.

Ahead I saw a solitary land mass that rose majestically from the ice-covered sea in the shape of a perfect cone. I stopped to check my map. It was Allard Island, a four-hundred-foot-high mountain, our destination for the day. The island had been a distinctive navigational landmark for the past few hours. As I put my map away Charlie lay resting. The day had been long and he was tired. I patted him, telling him that our campsite was just ahead a few miles. He seemed unimpressed, but rose slowly to his feet anyway, and together we started out.

With the somber cliffs behind us and wide-open space around us, the oppressive isolation that had engulfed me in the fjord now dissipated. My spirits perked up, pleased at the prospect of traveling thirty-five miles in one day. Finally, much to Charlie's relief, we arrived at the tip of Allard Island at eight o'clock, just in time to make the scheduled radio call to base camp. Taking my skis off, I climbed the six-foot slope and found a handy flat spot to pitch the tent. It would be a welcome change to camp on solid land instead of the sea ice that normally creaked and groaned with the rising and falling tides beneath my tent. As the sun slipped below the horizon the temperature dropped to minus 21 degrees. While I made the radio call a tired Charlie, without waiting for dinner, curled up and fell fast asleep. Except for his passionate protest at not being allowed to follow the bear tracks, my faithful companion had plodded at my side without complaint, even as we covered thirty-five miles during a marathon day.

Chapter Nine —
Far From Anywhere

Although it was only four A.M the sun was well up in the cloudless, pale blue sky, and there was just a whisper of a breeze. Charlie was making it abundantly clear that it was breakfast time. After feeding him, I pulled my down parka on and took the map out to study the route ahead from where I stood on Allard Island. When making my final plans at base camp—to travel northwest from Allard to Sherard Osborn Island, then continue northwest to King Christian Island's far northern coastline, located on the northernmost edge of the Pole's region for the year—I knew the stretch from Osborn to King Christian would present the most challenging navigation of the whole journey. But this route would give me the advantage of traveling within the entire magnetic North Pole area, where I could record in detail all the islands that I would see and touch for the Adventure Classroom educational project.

I set to work to break camp while Charlie took the opportunity to take another nap. He was brilliant in his ability to conserve energy. He never stood when he could sit. He never sat when he could lie down, and short naps worked well for him. No wonder he could instantly turn into a dynamic ball of ferocious energy when the need arose.

By five o'clock we were headed northwest to Sherard Osborn, the last island before the route would take us across the seventy-mile stretch of ice-covered, nameless sea. Charlie suddenly spied an Arctic fox that darted away to hide behind a hummock of ice. Immediately getting into the spirit of a fox chase, he suddenly pulled hard to the right, sending me flying to land hard on the ice. With his lead attached to my waist harness, he kept pulling me and I went sliding over the ice. He apparently thought I was really getting into the spirit of the chase and kept pulling on his lead to get at the fox, which was by now well out of sight. I yelled, "Stop, Charlie!" He instantly stopped, but probably wondered, *What in the world is she doing? Doesn't she like to chase foxes?* Then, seeing an opportunity for a new game, he forgot about the fox. As I lay tangled on the ice, he bounced on me with his front feet, then spread himself across my chest while he shoved his wet nose into my face. I grabbed him around his thick neck and wrestled him onto his back. Now this large ninety-four-pound black furry dog and my skis and I were hopelessly tangled. I struggled to a sitting position and unclipped Charlie's lead, released my skis, and got to my feet, while

Charlie went off to see if he could locate the fox. I got myself back on my skis and called him to me. I was somewhat disgruntled by the whole episode and glad that no one had been around to see the tangled spectacle we must have presented. But Charlie was in good spirits and seemed not to regard the entire incident as a problem at all.

To take advantage of the good weather, I decided to ski until midnight. Weak sunlight filtered through a thin layer of high clouds as I skied onward. We were on the eastern tip of Sherard Osborn, where the fast-moving ocean currents had pushed the sea ice high into jagged piles.

I took out the map to plot our course north. From here we would head northwest, leaving the islands behind and navigating out of sight of land. I would have to measure distance carefully to keep track of my latitude and longitude on the map. The sled's odometer would give me distance traveled. With our position and course carefully plotted and all my navigation information and tools in place, we were now ready to set out across the nameless sea.

I looked ahead at the blank, landless space stretched before us, totally devoid of any distinguishing features. The ice glistened as I searched for something to focus on. But there was only bare ice in all directions until it met the distant horizon. In that vast empty space Charlie and I were two microscopic specks—tiny, almost invisible ants, making our way across the stark emptiness.

Optimistically I aimed to reach King Christian in two more days. At midnight, after a nineteen-hour day and thirty-five miles, we stopped to camp. Charlie made it abundantly clear that the day had been long enough. The moment I stopped he immediately lay squarely across my skis. His message was clear: *We are stopping for the day!* He didn't need to tell me twice. It was with heartfelt relief that I shed my sled harness and skis. I unfastened Charlie from his sled. Assured that his message had been heard, he moved off my skis and curled up in a tight ball to sleep between the two sleds. As far as he was concerned, our day had ended and he was not to be disturbed. A couple of times earlier in our journey, Charlie had signaled me by lying across my skis when he wanted to end the day, but this was his most emphatic message yet. After erecting the tent, I gave him his dinner. After a few quick gulps, in no time he was fast asleep on my sleeping bag, leaving me a narrow sliver of space into which I finally slid my tired body. I soon fell asleep listening to his soft, contented snores.

Next day we traveled hour after hour through an energy-sapping wind that by six that night had increased to close to twenty miles per hour. My goal was to travel until midnight again. A valiant Charlie kept up with the steady pace and showed no signs of lagging. It continued to amaze me that this dog, who had known only the typical life of an Inuit dog with no name and no human petting, was faithfully walking at my side to a place that would make no sense to him. And he was ready to defend me with his life. I reached down to pat his head and he looked up at me as if to say, *I'm with you all the way.*

Later, after that day that seemed at times without end, came the long-awaited hour of midnight with another thirty-four miles behind us. As soon as I put the tent up, Charlie walked through the door with a determined purpose to his stride. He lay down in the center of the floor and in his resolute way made it clear that he was done for the day. I fed Charlie his dinner, and after my usual no-frills quick meal I laid down my sleeping bag. Charlie immediately claimed half.

We were now on our eighteenth day and more than halfway through our journey. The dreaded wake-up time of four A.M. arrived all too soon. Although Charlie and I were both seriously sleep-deprived, the idea of seeing land again was the motivation I needed to pack everything and set out.

A still-sleepy Charlie exited the tent only when I allowed it to collapse around him. He emerged slowly from its folds and immediately curled up beside his sled to resume much-needed sleep. It was only after I had packed everything, put my sled harness and skis on, and clipped Charlie's harness to his sled that he consented to rise to his feet. I was thankful that he couldn't express his opinion concerning our travel arrangements and the resulting lack of sleep. I'd planned on leaving by five A.M. We left with five minutes to spare.

After two nights of only three hours of sleep, I felt like a skiing zombie. Suddenly Charlie stopped and rolled on the ice, after which he got to his feet and gave a mighty shake and we were off once more. I took it to be his way of shaking sleep out of his head. His method didn't appeal to me. Instead, I yawned my way through the first half-mile before I was fully awake.

By midmorning the hazy glare was in full force. I had grown tired of straining to see beyond the white light that reflected off everything, but I kept watching the northern horizon, searching for the land I knew had to be there.

Soon I saw the faint outline of land: King Christian. Rubbing the ice crystals off my eyelashes, I strained to see through the white glare. I headed toward the island, which now lay only three miles away. I was elated. I was on course. My careful navigation had paid off. There before us was the island I had wanted to see ever since deciding a few years ago to ski to the Pole.

The island seemed a silent, flat, desolate place that lay lonely and deserted in an ocean of ice. The land and sea ice met in a barely discernible line. Flat plates of two-foot-thick ice had ridden up in places over the land edge, pointing skyward at odd angles. The land was so low in elevation that it had been unable to stop the sea ice from invading its space. Rising only a few feet over a long distance inland, the island had the appearance of a crumpled white blanket. I had to judge the shore edge by the difference in the ice: the sea ice was cracked and buckled. In contrast, the land ice was more stable, giving less under my weight and without the hollow sound of the sea ice. Looking north, I saw a long coastline stretching to the northwest with no distinguishing features other than its own empty flatness.

The next plan was to travel north, the full length of the west coast, until we reached the far north coast, which lay at the northernmost edge of the magnetic North Pole region for the year. We would then travel south to locate the center of the Pole's area. After traveling through the center, we would then continue south to the southernmost edge of the magnetic North Pole expanse, close to Helena Island, to arrive at a prearranged aircraft pickup point well within the southern edge of the polar region. This would complete the circumnavigation of the entire magnetic North Pole environment that the Canadian Geological Survey scientists had determined to be the northern and southern boundaries for 1988.

We ate a long-overdue lunch before moving on. As soon as the food bag appeared, Charlie immediately concentrated his full attention on its contents. By now he had perfected his technique of begging to such a degree that I had to turn my back to resist those begging eyes. When I didn't respond, those same eyes revealed the deepest sorrow. I handed him half of my crackers and peanut butter cups, and I made do with an assortment of nuts. Sometimes I felt that I was merely accompanying Charlie on this journey. *Wasn't it supposed to be the other way around?* I thought, *oh well, between the two of us we're making good progress and we'll reach the Pole, so it doesn't really matter who's in charge.*

As I skied along the coastline, I still saw no real distinguishing features. The silence was overwhelming, so much so that I began talking to Charlie to break the hushed stillness. I explained the details of my navigation to get there. After I had covered all aspects of my route-finding, I talked to him about my dream of seeing the island, but soon ran out of anything to say about a landmass that was so unremarkable in appearance and so ominously silent. Charlie said nothing. He, as usual, plodded onward close at my side without any obvious emotion. I wondered what he would say if he could talk. Upon reflection, I thought it better that I not know. *He must surely wonder why I'm making such a fuss over arriving at a place with no redeeming qualities in the middle of nowhere.*

We had traveled only twenty miles, far short of the daily thirty-plus miles of the past few days. It looked as if the good weather would hold and an early camp would allow us to catch up on our sleep. While I erected the tent, Charlie lay down alongside his sled. With a deep contented sigh that made it clear that he was glad to stop, he promptly fell asleep.

The light wind that had been blowing steadily for the last few hours developed into sudden gusts that sent loose snow swirling high into the air. As I concentrated on threading poles into the tent sleeves, a strong gust sent a shiny object clattering and tumbling past my feet. Recognizing it as Charlie's pan, the only one he had, I dashed in desperate pursuit. Using my best running tackle, I lunged for it, but I was no match for the speeding pan, which quickly disappeared into the distance. My only reward was a face full of snow as I skidded face down to a stop. Not only was it his only pan, but I also used it to mix warm water and oatmeal with his dog food.

As I brushed a liberal layer of snow off my jacket and extracted even more from where it had been jammed down my neck, I wondered, *What would Charlie use now?* Of course, the answer was obvious. We would have to share mine. Although perhaps not an acceptable practice in polite society, sharing was all we could do out here where life was stripped of all civilized pretense. Besides, Charlie wouldn't mind using my bowl. I realized that my life had been reduced to the most basic requirements. Returning to my camp chores, I noticed that Charlie had not stirred or seemed to notice my wild dash after his pan. In the meantime, the wind had swung to the south and the clouds had darkened to signal an approaching storm. "Well, Charlie, at least we made it to the island before all hell breaks loose again," I told him. To make sure that nothing else would meet the same fate as Charlie's pan, I took extra time to tie everything down securely. The rising wind gusted to thirty miles per hour. Charlie had long since moved out of the wind and into the vestibule, where he lay curled up fast asleep.

I turned in early, and since we hadn't seen any bear tracks for the last twelve hours I allowed Charlie to sleep in the tent again, out of the blowing snow.

At two A.M. I awoke to the cheerful sound of almost no wind. The sky was clear, but the south wind was a persistent worry. Rather than wait until the usual wake-up hour of four A.M. I decided to take advantage of the calm conditions. We set off with the drifting south breeze at our backs and continued our way up the island's coastline. The deep silence and desolation had wrung all signs of life from the snow-covered gravel moonscape that stretched across gently rising slopes. Our sleds moved easily across the smooth ice. Charlie's tiny blue child's sled was almost empty. From the first day of our journey most of his food, extra collar, and chain had been stashed on my sled. Although his powerful physique was capable of pulling more, I needed him to remain fresh enough to stay alert and watchful for bear signs. We hadn't seen bear tracks for quite some time, which was a relief for me, but Charlie stopped occasionally and with raised nose checked for bear and seal scents that might drift in on the incoming air currents. Now and then, when a particularly strong scent floated in, he gazed intently into the distance—I assumed in eager anticipation of meeting more bears.

As the island's coastline unfolded to our right, there was no relief from the cold barren mood of the place. The sea ice along the shoreline was fragile, cracked, and broken. An apprehensive Charlie was hesitant to cross thin ice that barely held our weight. Sometimes he stopped and looked up at me as if to say, *Can't we find something a little more solid?*

Later, as we veered away from shore to avoid the precarious ice, the coast curved, then swept northwest to a place that, according to my map, was named Sutherland Point. It was a wide projection of flat land, so flat in places that it did not show a single wrinkle in its icy cover. Beyond a bay I could see the effects of tidal currents that had swept around the point. Floes of ice that pushed upward at steep angles forced me to swing wide—much to Charlie's relief—to find flat, thicker ice. At times the ice creaked and groaned around us like the timbers of an old ship. At other times, loud rifle-like cracks echoed around us. Any sound in the deep silence was magnified, causing me to jump at the slightest noise. There were thick slabs of ice that tilted at drunken angles, forcing detours. I wondered if the tide was cresting as we passed, causing the violent chaos and spine-chilling noise that emitted from deep within the ice. Concerned for a worried Charlie, I stopped to reassure him. But as we resumed walking, it was clear that he would be happy only when we left this coast behind.

As our journey unfolded, I had learned that Charlie's fine-tuned senses enabled him to detect not only the presence of polar bears long before I was aware of them, but also the danger of thin, unstable ice, and the presence of close-by open water, even when visibility was so bad that it was impossible for me to see more than an arm's length ahead. Later this day in a desperate situation, I would again be reminded of his valuable intuition.

We kept up a steady pace along the island's western shoreline and arrived at a place where the ice, only a few inches thick, had buckled and lay in broken, cracked floes several feet wide. Some had ridden over neighboring floes, while others had been pushed to almost vertical angles over twenty feet tall. I stepped gingerly onto the first reasonably flat floe, carefully trusting my full weight to it. Charlie was not a happy fellow. He pulled back and did not want to cross. I thought the route ahead looked safe and tugged on his lead until he followed slowly and reluctantly, balking at the cracks and gaps. But I was soon in trouble.

On a particularly steep sloping ice pan, my skis suddenly slipped sideways and unceremoniously dumped me on my side. I realized immediately that I was vulnerable to stepping through the thin ice and through holes hidden by a thin layer of snow. Hoping that my boots would gain a better grip on the slippery ice, I removed the skis and quickly tied them on top of my sled.

The ice moved and grated as we picked our way forward. Charlie cautiously tried to skirt the worst places. It was now clear to me that he had not wanted to cross this area of ice because he knew it was unsafe. I wished that I had listened to him and that I had his same intuition. But it was too late; we were in a position of no return and the only way out was to move forward to safer ice. Just as I was balancing myself with my ski poles to step around a particularly fragile area, my feet flew backward, slamming me face down on an ice pan that had tilted with Charlie's and my combined weight. With my sled pulling me down, I began sliding backward toward a gaping, water-filled crevasse. With an instinct born of desperation, I lunged for the top edge of the tilting ice pan. My left-hand fingers barely curled over the top to give me enough grip to hang on and stop my backward slide. With my right hand I reached out and grabbed a wildly scrambling Charlie who, with his front claws, was frantically trying to stop his own backward slide into the watery crevasse. With adrenaline-induced strength and a last-ditch shove from me, Charlie managed to get his claws over the top edge and pull himself and his sled up. Then, with a quick scramble, he jumped to the next flat floe. By now my floe, already at thirty degrees, was tilting at an ever-steepening angle with the weight of my sled and supplies, dragging me downward toward the water and threatening to pull my fingers free. With a quick look backward over my shoulder, I saw that the back end of my sled was already in the water. If I released my sled harness, I would lose everything, including the tent.

I was still sliding downward. The thought of landing in the frigid black water sent a new surge of adrenaline charging through my body. With my fingers desperately clutching the edge of the ice floe and my face close to the ice, inch by inch I pulled myself and my sled upward until, with a last desperate effort, I hooked my chin over the top. Using my neck muscles to hold me there, I grabbed the top with one hand and then used the other to gain a solid grip on the top edge of the floe. With a final heave upward, I hooked both elbows over the edge. As my weight moved higher, the top edge slowly dropped until it was almost level, overlapping the next floe, where Charlie was standing. Dragging my sled behind me, I scrambled on all fours to safety and sat on the ice exhausted, breathing deeply. I looked back and saw that the floe that had tilted under our weight had been balanced on the next floe, which had functioned as a seesaw under our combined weight and sleds.

Charlie leaned his full weight against me and gave me a quick face lick, then leaned even closer. I felt a little foolish. After all, if I had taken notice of Charlie's reluctance to cross that area of ice, we would have avoided trouble. But regardless of what he might have thought of my lack of good judgment, he was still right there at my side, as faithful as ever. There was no doubt in my mind that he had been aware of our close call with disaster. I had found strength far beyond my imagination. I was thankful for all the years of international discus throwing and luge competition, the weight training, and the previous two years of stringent physical preparation for this expedition. My mind wandered to thoughts of what would have happened to Charlie if I hadn't been able to get myself out of trouble. Shoving such depressing thoughts away, I stood and saw a route to the right that would work. I couldn't wait to get away from this topsy-turvy area of unstable ice. Another fifty feet took us to safer ice.

After deciding that wearing skis would be safer, I clipped them onto my boots and set off again, weaving my way forward through more unpredictable ice. I was spurred on to leave this area far behind us by the memory of the water-filled chasm snapping at my heels in anticipation of a victim and the possibility of Charlie disappearing into the icy depths.

Charlie, in his usual resolute way, walked close at my side. A half mile farther on we were on smoother, thicker ice, allowing me to take a long, relieved breath, knowing that at last we could leave the horror behind us. I resolved that from now on I would trust Charlie's judgment when he seemed to question my route-finding. His reluctance to follow my choice of route was due to a lifetime of traveling across sea ice, which had given him the ability to discern the difference between safe and unsafe ice. He had sensed the danger before we stepped on the seesaw ice. He had even jerked his head away when I pulled on his lead. The whole episode was a lesson I would not forget. As we headed north, I wondered what else he could teach me if he could speak—much more, I suspected.

We had traveled only seventeen miles that day. Our episode with the shoreline ice had made the miles seem longer. It was only four-thirty, but I decided to camp opposite the hills and prepare for careful navigation tomorrow. I had just finished putting my tent up when I heard the faint sound of an approaching aircraft. I looked south to see a Twin Otter airplane flying at low altitude straight toward us. Raising my arms above my head, I waved in excitement and gave them a thumbs-up signal to tell them that Charlie and I were okay. After so long without seeing any sign of other humans, it was a thrill to see the pilot and passengers waving to us as they swooped low just above our heads. They circled again, and the roar of the plane's engines sliced the Arctic's silence. Dipping the wings in a final salute, the plane gained altitude and continued northward as I watched it disappear into the hazy distance. Its powerful roar was replaced by the heavy weight of silence. The plane and its occupants reminded me that Charlie and I were completely isolated from anyone and that it had been a long time since we had had any human contact. Later, after our return to base camp, I met the pilot, Roger Greene, an Australian. I learned that he had been flying a group of scientists and engineers to the far north to collect samples in their study of the Arctic environment and had been told by Bezal of our journey. He told me that Charlie and I had looked terribly alone, surrounded by a white, endless space that looked as if it could engulf us.

We had reached the northern coast of King Christian Island and the most northerly boundary of the magnetic North Pole. To record the event, I decided to take a photo of Charlie and me standing alongside our tent with the northern hills of King Christian Island in the background. I set the camera on its tripod before calling Charlie, who was stretched out asleep on my sleeping bag. When there was no response to my call, I looked into the tent and called again. Still no response! He didn't even look up. Photography was not on his schedule, at least not today. Only something special would persuade him to leave his comfortable bed. With a lot of noisy rattling, I took the stove and saucepan out of my sled and pretended to begin cooking a meal. Charlie rose and peeked outside to check on the proceedings, but when no food was offered, he quickly lost interest and returned to my sleeping bag. He was too wise to fall for my trickery. Only his favorite peanut butter cups and crackers would do. Once I laid a handful of each on the ice outside the door, he immediately rose and stepped outside to gobble down the lot.

By the time I set the timer and focus for the photo, he had already disappeared inside the tent to resume his sleep. I grabbed his lead and urged him outside again, and after I had pushed him into an acceptable sitting position, I ran to the camera and was successful in pressing the shutter twice for two photos before he disappeared into the depths of the tent once more. *Oh well,* I thought, *two photos are better than none.* I could tell by Charlie's determined return to my sleeping bag that he considered posing for photos to be some sort of torturous penance.

That night's base camp call brought the unwelcome news that a severe storm with exceptionally high winds was approaching from the south. Our next task was to travel thirty miles south to the coordinates in the center of the magnetic Pole's region. If only the weather would cooperate until we reached it.

Engulfed in the storm

Digging out

Chapter Ten —
The Storm

Around midnight, lenticular clouds—some cigar-shaped and others shaped like saucers—all signaled approaching strong winds. The temperature had risen five degrees, and the south wind had increased to ten miles per hour.

I broke camp and we started the journey south at one A.M. My plan was to ski farther out from the coastline to escape the dangerous coastal ice of King Christian, then continue south to reach the central coordinates of the Pole in one long day.

As we headed south, Charlie easily kept pace in his usual place at my right side. We arrived at the southern tip of King Christian, and I stopped for one last look at the most surreal, lonely island I had ever seen. As a landmass it was an understatement, but I would always remember it. During all my expedition planning I had longed to see the island. Its northern coast represented the most northerly boundary of the polar region for the year and had been my northernmost point, and now it seemed strange that I was leaving it behind, splendidly alone, silent, with no sign of life anywhere. I finally turned away to concentrate on the task of navigating across the same blank landless space we had traveled across on our way north. After taking careful directional checks of the sun and wind, I headed south. Our destination was only nineteen miles away.

By four in the morning a towering wall of blue-black billowing clouds, stretching many miles across, was building in intensity as it approached from the far south. The wide, uninterrupted horizon enabled me to see the entire storm front in one view that was overwhelming in its sheer size and power. Increasingly strong gusts of wind swirled snow high into the air. Later, before the sun disappeared behind the dark clouds, I took various directional checks that confirmed that I was right on course. But navigation was a minor problem compared to the towering wall of dense clouds that continued to roll toward us.

Skiing at a pace of two miles per hour, we were closing in on the Pole. But sometime after four o'clock, I saw to my horror that a roiling mass of thick clouds was racing low across the ice straight at us. Realizing that we were about to be trapped in a colossal storm of gigantic proportions, I unclipped my skis and sled harness and ran to my sled. It was impossible to erect the tent. Charlie and I would have to shelter behind the sled. But first I needed to anchor everything securely to the ice so that my sled and its contents wouldn't be swept into oblivion.

Next, I ran with Charlie to the sheltered side of the sled and anchored his lead into the ice. I shoved my arms into my down parka and stuffed my mitts into the pockets. Then I grabbed the tent and grasped the sled tie-down rope to tighten it just as the wind, with the sound of an approaching jet, bore down on us with a force so great I struggled to stand upright. Clutching the tent to my chest, I scrambled toward the sheltered side of the sled, but had taken only a step or two when the wind blasted into my body, sending me crashing face down to the ice with such bone-jarring force that my goggles were knocked off. Half blinded by flying snow and chunks of ice, I first thought of Charlie, expecting to see him airborne. To my relief, I saw that the ice screw anchoring his lead held fast. He was hunkered down behind the sled, which protected him from the missiles of ice that were flying like bullets through the air. Barely able to see, with eyes blasted by flying ice particles, I scrambled and slithered for cover, keeping low to avoid being hit by more chunks of ice in the rising force of the howling wind. I crashed into Charlie's side, out of breath and half blind. Then through the wild pandemonium I saw my gear being sucked out of the sled. Crawling on all fours I fought through the wind, which by now had reached a high-pitched scream, to grab the loose tie-down rope and jerk it tight. Still clutching the tent to my chest, I dived over the top of my sled, and as fast as I could I wrapped the tent around both of us and put my arm around Charlie, more to comfort myself than him. As usual, he was calm, but he ducked down low to avoid being hit by airborne ice. Our surroundings were being plunged into premature night as the storm blocked out the sun. I could see no more than a couple of paces in all directions. We were locked into a raging bubble of violence. Crouching low behind the sled, I felt blood trickling down my face. When my goggles had been knocked off, my face and one eye had been blasted by flying ice. My eye was swollen almost shut. I couldn't tell how bad the cuts were, and I prayed that the damage wasn't serious.

The sled took the full force of the wind, but the wind's long arms reached over and around, clawing at the tent, trying to rip it from my grasp. I held on tight with both hands, determined to keep our only shelter intact. Trapped and cramped with no ability to move around behind the sled, my worry now was that the storm and the freezing cold might last long enough to drive my body into hypothermia. Under hypothermic conditions Charlie would last longer than I would. A frightening thought loomed through my worry: *What will happen to Charlie if I don't survive?* According to the calculations I had taken before being swallowed up by the storm, we were only two miles from the Pole's center.

To help my bleeding eye remain closed more easily, I smoothed one of the candy wrappers, placed it over my eye, and wound a draw cord from the inside of my jacket around my head and over the wrapper so that my eye would be protected, pirate style. At least it would be a temporary measure until I could get to my first aid kit, which I hoped had not been swept away to goodness-knew-where in the wind. Now the only thing Charlie and I could do was sit out the storm and hope that it wouldn't last too long. I sat with my head on my bent knees and felt blood trickling down my face. A boiling mass of clouds hung over us, as if trying to crush us into the ice. The jet-like noise was deafening. It wasn't long before deep cold began to creep into my body and I started to shiver.

To my amazement, Charlie curled up at my side and went to sleep, seemingly oblivious to the screaming chaos that continued to trap us in its furious grasp. How could he sleep under these conditions and appear so unworried? *Oh well,* I thought briefly, *perhaps I should take my cue from him and do the same.* But I immediately knew that would be impossible. To survive I had to find some way to keep whatever warmth I had. I wriggled my toes and fingers, and moved my arms and legs as much as possible within the confines of the tiny space I crouched in. Time crawled by in slow motion as the increasing cold continued its relentless journey throughout my body. My shivering intensified, and my hands and feet gradually succumbed to the cold. Food would have helped, but it was impossible to stand in the wind, much less look for my food bags. An hour passed and still there was no escape. The storm continued to blast our world, hurling snow and ice horizontally at us, reducing visibility to almost zero. My movements became stiffer and slower and I shivered less, a bad sign. Hypothermia was well on its way. I fought back with isometric exercises and even mental arithmetic. *Two times two equals four*, all the way to *sixteen times sixteen equals two hundred and fifty-six*. But no matter how hard I fought I knew that I was losing the battle. The intense cold marched onward throughout my body. Nothing seemed to stop its slow but steady progress.

Charlie, in spite of the chaos that surrounded us, slept on. After an hour I woke him to make sure he was not succumbing to hypothermia. All I got was one sleepy eye opening just enough to see that we weren't going anywhere, and back to sleep he went. He wasn't suffering from the cold as I was and seemed perfectly happy to sleep the storm away. Even the relentless screaming of high-pitched gusts seemed not to disturb him. Staying as low as possible, I continued to crouch alongside Charlie. The wind pounded the sled so hard it jerked and shuddered as if alive.

Another hour passed and suddenly I realized that the wind seemed quieter and I no longer could hear the howl of approaching gusts. Or could it be my imagination? Were my prayers being answered? My body ached with the cold and I could hardly think anymore. My movements were slow and sluggish. I peeked out from under the tent fabric, and to my delight I saw a glimmer of sun as it fought its way through the thick gray clouds. If I'd had the energy, I would have whooped with joy. My eye was painful and swollen shut. I felt dried blood on my face. But I concentrated on going through the painful process of standing upright and getting some warmth back into my body. The wind still tugged at us, but at least it wasn't knocking me over now, and I wasn't being greeted by soaring chunks of ice.

I was so cold and stiff I could only get to my knees, then haul myself up slowly. Every joint protested. It was as if the cold had welded my joints together. I walked in circles, windmilling my arms to force blood into my numb fingers. I marched in place, working warmth back into my legs and feet. At first, I moved in painful slow motion, but warmth gradually inched its way back. It took some time, but at last my body, although not really warm, was an immensely improved version of the cold, stiff bundle that had huddled desperately behind the sled.

Charlie awoke, stretched, and walked to the end of his lead to attend to nature. Next, he calmly sat and waited expectantly for food as if nothing out of the ordinary had occurred. He wasn't in the least perturbed by what we had just gone through and acted as if it were all just another day in the Arctic. In contrast, I was relieved that we had both survived the ordeal. How I envied him his understanding of the extremes of his homeland.

I began putting the tent up, at the same time noticing that the wind was gradually increasing. Another wall of blowing snow, still several miles away, was bearing down on us. I tried to hurry, but my fingers were still slow and my body, which seemed burdened by an extraordinary weight, wouldn't listen to my mind urging it on. Snow, picked up by the increasing wind, billowed into the air. I feared that I wouldn't get the tent up in time, but my body finally kicked in, warming as I shook the great weight off and regained strength. Now pure, raw desire to survive took over. I had already anchored one end of the tent even before beginning to erect it, to prevent a possible untimely exit. I shoved poles into pole sleeves, working furiously to beat the approaching wall of clouds. One blast almost turned the tent inside out, and I was afraid a pole would break. Finally, a combination of poles, ice screws, and tie-down ropes anchored the tent to the ice. I hurried around adding as many tie-downs as possible, then invented more until I had no rope left. I dragged my sled into the tent and propped it against one wall to help brace against the wind, then attached

Charlie's sled to an ice screw just outside. As the high-pitched scream of the wind drew closer, I ran to Charlie, rushing him into the back of the tent. After one last check that all was secure, I dove through the doorway. I grabbed an emergency belay rope and tied one end around my waist and another to Charlie's harness. Then, as fast as I could, I hooked the rope to an ice screw just outside the doorway so that if the tent were swept away Charlie and I wouldn't go tumbling across the ice after it. Zipping the door closed as much as the rope allowed, I scrambled to lean against the wall opposite my sled and braced myself for the shrieking blast I could hear bearing down on us. There was a sudden eruption as the tent was laid almost flat. The specially made poles snapped upright again with no apparent damage. But I wondered how much punishment they could take before bending or breaking. With my feet braced against my sled, I fought with all my strength to brace the windward wall.

In the back of the tent even the usually calm Charlie sat bolt upright, alarmed at the loud snapping noise the tent walls made as they convulsed back and forth. This was a new experience for him. He was used to surviving storms without shelter or protection of any kind, but now the added clamor of the tent had his full attention. After a few minutes he relaxed and leaned back against the wall in complete comfort, which helped stabilize the back floor and wall. After a couple of particularly thunderous blasts, he started toward me as if to seek assurance that everything was all right, but I urged him back to his place in the rear. He obeyed, but looked uneasy and kept sending me looks that made it clear that he was unhappy and felt very insecure. Then it was impossible for me to resist beckoning him. In an instant he was right beside me, pressed firmly into my side. Although I knew that for the sake of the tent's survival he should stay back, his closeness was a comfort to me, and judging by the way he relaxed against my side, my nearness gave him added confidence. I put my arm around him as I listened to the racket that surrounded us. A deafening roar hit us again and I was certain that this time the tent would give in. But although the tent anchors were tested to the limit, and the tent fabric snapped violently, everything held. The din went on and on until I wondered aloud to Charlie if it would ever stop. At least I was thankful that I could sit upright, which was preferable to crouching low on the ice behind my sled.

An hour crawled by and the powerful gusts that had been surging in, one after the other, slowly began to give way to increasingly long lulls. Although the wind still lifted snow high into the air and snapped at the tent, it was bearable compared to the maelstrom we had just survived. It seemed that at least for now, the real danger of being blown away had passed. Then, finally, only stray gusts swept in as if reluctant to leave. As the outside din lessened, Charlie lay down with his head on my lap and dozed off. For him the excitement was over, and it was time for a quick nap. But sleep was far from my mind. Moving Charlie off my lap, I looked out to see that the clouds were still heavy overhead, blocking the light, leaving only a solid grayness. My inspection of the tent showed the only damage to be a torn-out tie-down grommet. The low profile and modern design of the tent had won out. But how much food and equipment had been swept away? I unzipped the sled bag. My worst fears were realized. My sleeping mat, crampons, extra stove, and assorted odds and ends were gone, but I could continue without those. Most of the stove fuel had blown away, so water would be severely restricted. That was serious. After a search for Charlie's food, I discovered that half had disappeared, which meant half rations for him from now on. But he had eaten well throughout the journey, enjoying both his and my food, and had actually gained weight, so I knew that he would be safe on half rations. He could go back to eating ice rather than drinking water, as he had done all of his life before this journey. Inuit dogs are used to frequent periods of starvation and have learned over many generations to survive under conditions much harsher than the ones we faced now.

Once I had assured myself that Charlie would be safe, I turned to searching for my own food. At first I found none, but then remembered the bag where I kept my daytime traveling snacks such as peanut butter cups, crackers, and nuts. With fingers that fumbled with anxiety, I opened the green nylon sack and found a few walnuts. I counted out seven small handfuls of five walnuts for each of the next seven days it would take us to reach the prearranged aircraft pickup place at Helena Island. There was enough fuel to melt ice for one pint of water per day, but it would have to do. Not much compared to the two or three quarts I had been drinking each day. Now the question was, did I have enough food and water to survive in this extremely dry and cold climate? I understood the realities of going from five thousand calories a day to less than one hundred calories, combined with very little water and several days of hard work ahead of us. Fighting hunger and thirst and the resulting weakness would make it difficult to travel the remaining miles, but I knew it could be done. Charlie had enough food to make it safely. I was confident that we could finish our journey, but I knew I would be in for some hard times.

I took out my signal mirror to inspect the damage to my face and eyes. Both eyes were bruised black and swollen almost shut. I looked as if I had just come away from the losing end of a prizefight. I covered my right eye with a medicated eye patch from my first aid kit and hoped a night's sleep would improve it. I was hungry, but I would have to wait until tomorrow to eat and drink. The first priority was to get a good night's sleep, in hopes that the weather would cooperate and allow us to leave early in the morning. I unloaded my sleeping gear and threw it in the tent. After I carefully measured Charlie's half ration of dog food, he ate it in the tent, then curled up in his favorite spot beside my sleeping bag and was fast asleep in minutes. The temperature had climbed to 16 degrees above zero, an incredible change and no doubt a large factor in the storm. The wind had calmed down and it began to snow. "If there are any bears around out there," I told the sleeping Charlie, "they'll have to wait until morning." I was so tired from all that we had been through that for once I really didn't care about bears. I was just glad to have survived that hellish day in one piece.

Day twenty-one arrived and the first thing I noticed when I awoke at six A.M. was the peaceful, but uncanny silence. It was snowing lightly. My right eye was swollen shut and I could barely see out of my left eye.

I took Charlie for a short walk around the tent site to see if travel was at all achievable, but low visibility and my eye problems seemed likely to make it impossible. The temperature was still plus 16 degrees, the highest by far of the entire journey, but it was snowing and the poor visibility was made worse by my eye problem. I returned to the tent with a heavy heart. My fear of hunger said that somehow, we had to get going: I simply didn't have enough food and fuel to wait long. It was tempting to pack up and push ahead, but I knew that wasn't safe. With very limited eyesight, how would I deal with a polar bear, and would I see gaps in the ice in time to prevent Charlie and me from falling through? The answer was a definite no. All we could do was wait patiently for a change.

Around ten A.M. I looked out at a ghostly scene. It had stopped snowing, but the visibility was cut down even further with the arrival of dense fog that had quietly crept in and covered everything in a dismal gray blanket of silence. Charlie sat in the doorway for a while and then, having apparently decided that we weren't going anywhere, and ever the one to sensibly conserve energy, he curled up and with a contented sigh fell asleep. Looking at him, I decided that he had the right idea.

Shortly before noon I awoke to see a weak sun shining through the sides of the tent. A light southerly breeze had sprung up and the fog had rolled away just as silently as it had arrived. Visibility was good enough. If I squinted with my left eye, I could see far enough ahead to be reasonably safe. We were only two miles from the Pole's center.

After eating my day's ration of walnuts, which didn't satisfy the hunger that had begun the night before, I put on my spare set of goggles, which had darker lenses, to better protect my eyes. I was thankful for my habit of always carrying a spare set on expeditions.

Charlie was already up and ready to go. He stood at the side of his sled, and with a few sharp, impatient barks he signaled that it was time to leave. While I put my skis and sled harness on, he eagerly urged me forward with a few even louder barks. "Okay, Charlie, I'm coming," I told him as I fumbled with ski bindings that I could barely see. Charlie, in his anxiety to get going, pulled out in front, and with my reduced eyesight he almost pulled me off balance. I pulled him back to walk in his usual place at my right side and told him, "No pulling, just walking." We set off at a good pace, and after a few minutes we both settled down to our usual two-mile-per-hour cadence.

I kept checking the counter on my sled's odometer. At last, it read two miles, confirming that we had reached our destination. I confirmed our position at the center of the magnetic North Pole region with a satellite reading from my GPS unit and then called base camp to tell them that I had arrived at the Pole's central position.

Terry gave an enthusiastic "Yippee, congratulations! That's really great. Bill called and sends his love. We've been worried about the weather up your way. Are you okay?" I had already decided not to tell them about my limited food and water supply and the problems with my eyes. I was on the last leg of our journey, and I could see no reason to worry everyone now. I could tell them the whole story when I returned.

"A storm passed through and blew us around a bit, but we're okay now," I said, hoping I sounded convincing. "Please tell Bill I made it and I send my love."

That I was the first woman to reach the Pole on a solo expedition was not as important to me as was the opportunity to launch Adventure Classroom with this expedition. Now all that was left of this long journey was a final dash to our prearranged plane pickup point.

I hugged Charlie in celebration. He showed no unusual excitement. I'm sure the blank sheet of ocean ice that we stood on far from land seemed no different from the many he had seen all his life. But although I was the first woman to make this journey alone, it was also a special day for Charlie. He had also entered into Polar history. He was the first dog to have traveled as a lone dog to the Pole. All other dogs had been members of sled-pulling dog teams, a far different experience than Charlie's journey.

Our arrival at the Pole meant that we had to have photos of the occasion. First, I tied the national flag to my ski pole and planted it in the ice, then led Charlie to stand beside the flag. I returned to the camera only to find that Charlie had decided the time had arrived for an icy back scratch. All I could see through the lens was Charlie on his back, four feet in the air, wiggling back and forth—definitely not the dignified image I had in mind. I urged him to stand upright alongside the flag, but it was to no avail. He had no interest in my photography plans, so I gave up and set the shutter timer so that I could hold the flag with Charlie standing at my side. Now that the formalities of having arrived at the center of the Pole's region were over, we could stay no longer. The lack of food and water and the realities of what lay ahead of us in the coming days—before we could reach our pickup point—were vivid in my mind. Realizing that time lost now could spell trouble later, I rechecked my navigation and set out on a southeasterly course, intending to reach the aircraft pickup point located within the accepted southern edge of the Pole region. I now aimed for the center of Helena Island, thirty-five miles to the south, which according to the map consisted of high coastal northern cliffs that I hoped would be visible from several miles away. After we reached it, we would take a more easterly course to its eastern tip, where I hoped to find an area of smooth ice suitable for our pickup plane to land. This would complete the roughly triangular circumnavigation of the entire Pole area.

My eye problems forced me to ski at a vastly reduced speed as I groped my way forward. This, and my lack of supplies, would drastically cut into my energy and therefore into my daily mileage. I had allowed for seven days, but in the back of my mind I hoped that if all went well, perhaps I could make it in five. Although my eyes were in no shape to travel, I had no time to wait for them to heal.

My thirst increased as the extreme dryness of the Arctic air pulled moisture from my body. Rationing my water, I decided to save the last mouthful until camp that night as a treat. A gnawing hunger added to my problems, but I could do nothing about it. I had eaten my day's allotment of walnuts, so I would have to wait until tomorrow to eat again. With so little food and water I knew the next few days would be a race against starvation and dehydration.

I guessed the wind to be somewhere around twenty miles an hour and getting stronger. We had covered about three miles, but my eyes had had enough for the day. I groped around, setting up camp more by feel than anything else. My eyes worried me. I tried to look at them in the signal mirror but couldn't even see that close up. My real worry came when I realized that I wouldn't be able to fire the rifle or the flare gun with any accuracy. My eyes needed rest, and I would just have to trust Charlie to deal with any bear encounters. I patted Charlie goodnight and climbed wearily into my sleeping bag. The best cure for my eyes was sleep.

Frozen mask

Chapter Eleven —
Desperate March

Next morning at five A.M., although my eyes had improved, I was discouraged to see that we were engulfed in a thick gray fog that pressed silently in on all sides. Visibility was no more than a few feet. There was nothing to do but retreat to the haven of my sleeping bag to rest my eyes while I waited.

When Charlie saw that I wasn't preparing for travel, he moved all the way into the tent and, having decided that my legs would make an excellent pillow, laid his heavy head across my body and promptly fell asleep. His gentle snores were the only sound. It struck me as almost amusing that here we were stuck in dense fog far from any other humans in a vast vacuum of silence, and the only sound came from this big black dog as he slept.

A couple of hours later I decided to light the stove to melt water. After moving Charlie aside so that I could get up, he promptly moved over to lay along the full length of our bed. He had already figured out that we weren't going anywhere—so why not take advantage of the now-vacant sleeping bag?

By the time I had filled my thermos with water and eaten a few walnuts, a light southerly breeze had sprung up to gradually drive the blanket of fog away, revealing a clear path through the rutted ice ahead. While I packed my sled, Charlie reluctantly left the comfort of the sleeping bag and lay on his back for his customary tummy rub. Then with a body-consuming shake and a couple of sharp barks he announced that he was ready to leave. We set out before noon under a canopy of thin, broken clouds and sun that was patchy at best. The weather seemed locked into a pattern of southerly winds with the possibility of more storms.

I kept my still-swollen right eye covered, but even with goggles my left eye quickly deteriorated in the bright light. Soon I looked through a one-eyed hazy curtain. To add to our problems, a rapidly increasing wind sent snow swirling about us in a dense white mass. Traveling slowly, I peered ahead, trying to will my ailing eyes to see as they teared up with the strain. Desperate to cover more miles, I forced myself ahead, but it wasn't long before my inability to see and avoid large chunks of ice made it impossible to stay upright. Frustration and desperation set in as I skied slower and slower. Taking my skis off to prevent a fall over some unseen lump of ice, I walked, knowing that each mile I covered was one mile closer to my destination. My left eye was running and the swirling snow was blinding, but I kept on. It wasn't long before I could hardly see at all, but rather than stop, I laid my hand on Charlie's back. If we came to an obstacle, I knew he would go around it and I would follow at his side. Not only was he my early-warning polar bear detection system, he had now become my seeing-eye dog, while the southerly wind was my direction-finder.

Charlie was a champion. He stayed at my side just as he had for the last twenty-one days. When I stopped, he stopped. After all those days and miles, he knew the routine and kept on. Our progress was notable for my slow clumsiness, but at least we were moving ahead. *Much better than sitting in the tent fretting about going nowhere,* I thought. I tried not to worry about meeting another bear. Charlie would react in his usual manner, but I wouldn't see it until it would perhaps be too late. There was no point in allowing my imagination to dwell on bears, so I shoved negative thoughts aside and concentrated on following Charlie as he led us onward.

After another five hours with Charlie's help, I had groped my way through less than three miles. But, I reasoned, we were at least making progress and every mile covered was one less. Side by side, Charlie and I continued through the icy obstacle course. Later, disappointed by our abysmally slow progress, I stopped for the day. Wearily, I calculated that over the last two hours we had covered less than a mile.

Erecting the tent was a circus act in itself. By now my abused eyes were so bad that even when I held the tent poles three inches from my face, I could barely see them. Finally, after I used an ingenious system of guessing and feel, the tent stood in a reasonably functional fashion. I invited Charlie into the tent. My eyesight predicament and the surrounding almost-zero visibility had reduced my world to a diameter of only a few feet.

Deeply disappointed with my progress, plagued with almost nonfunctioning eyes, the full impact of our extreme isolation far from any people hit me once I sat down to rest. I felt irrevocably alone on the planet. More than ever, I kept Charlie close at my side so that I could touch him and take comfort from his quiet, confident serenity. Of course, whenever Charlie was invited into the tent, he assumed that the invitation included the use of my sleeping bag. He seemed oblivious to the fact that I needed more than the two-inch strip he left me to slide into. To make matters worse, he had by now discovered the small pillow I had so carefully sewn at home to provide a minor but important measure of comfort to the whole journey. I pushed a protesting Charlie over to gain another inch or two, but as I squeezed my body into the remaining sleeping bag space, I found myself having to share my pillow. Charlie's big black head lay squarely in the middle, leaving only a corner for me.

Furthermore, his soft snores indicated that he was sound asleep. I had two choices. I could move him, which I knew from past experience would not be an easy task, or I could be grateful for the space left for me. I decided to take the easy route. I slid my body into the bag, positioned my head alongside Charlie's, and fell asleep. Sometime during the night Charlie awoke and moved, giving me the opportunity to reclaim my precious pillow, and I slept well until four A.M., awaking to yet another typical windy Arctic day. Although the sky was streaked with clouds, the sun was shining and there was no sign of the lenticular clouds that would signal another storm. The swelling around my eyes had almost disappeared, and to my relief my eyesight had significantly improved.

Breakfast consisted of a few walnuts (surprise!) and half my day's water, leaving the rest of my day's allotted supply for later. My hunger and raging thirst could no longer be ignored. I fed Charlie his breakfast and looked at his food with added interest. But I knew that even in my increasingly weak, hungry, and thirsty state, I couldn't in all good conscience take any of his food, especially now that he was on half rations. I hadn't asked him if he wanted to travel at my side over all these miles through storms, uncertain ice conditions, polar bears, and other dangers to a place that was unknown to him. Yet without complaint, he'd stayed close at my side, protecting me from the bears while demonstrating his total loyalty and trust in me. Even on half rations he was his usual energetic, enthusiastic self. We were a team. I felt a twinge of guilt that I had even a fleeting thought of sharing his food. One reason I pulled my own sled loaded with not only my gear and supplies but also almost all of Charlie's, was that I wanted to reach the Pole using my own energy, not that of a dog team or machine. Sharing even one bite of his food would have been a betrayal of not only Charlie's faithfulness but also my personal goals and expedition ethics.

I broke camp and set off hunching into a chill southeast wind. Navigation was simple. All I had to do was ski straight into the wind with only an occasional stop to check sun and wind direction. Charlie's paws and my boots and skis disappeared beneath the long fingers of a layer of blowing snow that slid straight at us across the icy surface. More snow billowed into the air, plastering our bodies in a white layer that froze to my clothing but slid off Charlie's much more functional coat. With heads down we forced our way ahead toward the northern cliffs of Helena Island, which were hidden beyond the wall of windblown snow. Unrelenting strong winds had dogged us for much of this journey. I was reminded of Bezal's description of the route I had followed to the Pole. "It's nothing but a wind tunnel," he had said in his no-nonsense, direct manner. "I hope you have a good tent; you'll need it."

With hunger and thirst dominating each mile, Helena Island seemed so far away. Thirst was an increasing problem, even more than the hunger that had begun to gnaw at me. In the dry Arctic air, I lost moisture with each breath. My allotted water supply wasn't enough to keep me going, so I resorted to eating snow. But the snow in that desert-like dryness holds little moisture and did nothing to alleviate my thirst. I chopped ice and placed small chunks on top of my sled, where I could reach back and grab them as I traveled. The searing cold of the ice raised blood blisters inside my mouth, but as I grew desperate for more fluid, I did my best to ignore them. I was tempted to drink the last half of my day's water supply, but I knew that I had to find the discipline somehow to save it for tonight and to eat ice during the day. The ever-resourceful Charlie, who had eaten ice all his life, saw my supply as a handy source for his own use. *Why dig for my own when a nicely chopped pile is within easy reach on top of her sled?* At one point I reached back, expecting to grab another icy morsel, only to find that there was none left. Charlie was noisily crunching the last piece. I marveled that he seemed to not experience any discomfort as he chewed, while my mouth ached from the intense cold. He was unquestionably more suited to the Arctic climate than his companion. I stopped to chop more ice. Charlie immediately joined in and dug with enthusiastic zeal alongside me. His fervent efforts sent the pieces I had chopped flying across the ice. I gave him a piece large enough that he would need time to chew it while I continued to chop chunks into small bite-sized pieces that I laid on top of my sled. The supply was large enough for us both. Having developed a preference for a ready-made ice supply, he took full advantage as we traveled onward and snatched a choice piece whenever the need arose.

 Hour after hour Charlie and I plodded onward. Head down, I forced my way through the wall of wind, breathing harder and losing even more moisture with each exhaled breath. Charlie pressed on in his usual stoic fashion, even when his face became encrusted in snow and ice. With each passing hour the wind increased. In spite of the brutal conditions, I resisted the urge to make camp and forced my skis to keep pushing ahead. But it wasn't long before my steps slowed. The now-constant gnawing ache in my stomach and my increasingly dry mouth made me long for even a small sip of water and a single mouthful of food. A few walnuts weren't sufficient for this hour-after-hour slogging work. I had no choice but to make do. I found it to be a decided advantage to accept what I had and feel grateful for it rather than wish I had more. Wishing only made me feel hungrier and thirstier, whereas acceptance and gratitude for what I had allowed me to channel my energy into moving ahead at a good pace. And as long as Charlie was fine, there was no reason to even consider quitting. After all, arriving at our destination would solve my problem.

 The afternoon wore on as the wind continued to strengthen. I decided that if the wind made it impossible to erect my tent, I could sleep in my sled if I had to. I clipped Charlie's lead to the back of my harness to enable him to walk behind me so that my body broke the full force of the wind and provided him some protection.

The sun slowly sank in the west, and still the wind continued to blow in our faces. Just before eight o'clock I stopped to make my daily radio call to base camp. Even though the wind made it almost impossible to erect the antenna, I persisted. As soon as Charlie saw that we were stopped, he lost no time in curling up to sleep on the ice, sheltered behind my sled. With a gentle nudge I woke the sound-asleep Charlie and hitched his harness to his almost empty sled. With a wide yawn and half-hearted stretch, he stood and we resumed our steady slog southeast. It was clear that he was tired and would have welcomed an end to this seemingly years-long day, but I told him, "Charlie, we have to keep going." He made no response, but perhaps in his canine wisdom he could sense our desperate need to persist in spite of the awful conditions that worsened by the hour. Just before midnight, after almost twenty hours and twenty-one miles of fighting the steadily deteriorating elements, I decided to end the struggle. After wolfing down his dinner, Charlie, clearly relieved to lie down for some undisturbed rest, fell asleep even before I had begun to unload the sled.

The risk of the tent turning into a kite in the wind (which frequently gusted to thirty miles an hour) convinced me to forgo the tent and grab a few hours of sleep in the sled instead. I positioned the two sleds so that Charlie could sleep between the two, sheltered from the wind. After consuming the last of my day's ration of a few walnuts and a couple of mouthfuls of water, I checked the tie-down anchors at each end of my sled, maneuvered around various items, and stretched my five-foot-three-inch frame into a reasonably comfortable position in my sleeping bag. Not exactly deluxe accommodations, but like Charlie, I was relieved to be out of the elements.

In spite of the maddening roar of the wind and my cramped quarters, hunger, and thirst, I fell into an exhausted dreamless sleep.

It was now day twenty-four. If only the weather would cooperate, we should reach our final destination in two or three days.

At two A.M. I awoke to find that a light gray fog had silently crept in to create a ghostlike mood. Visibility was all of six feet, but I decided to head out in the hopes of gaining at least a few miles. I climbed out of my sled, glad to leave my cramped cocoon. But my optimism evaporated even before I could clip my skis to my boots: it began to snow so heavily that visibility was cut to zero. Now frustrated almost beyond endurance, I erected the tent and prepared to wait for improved conditions. After feeding Charlie and melting a little ice for my meager allotment of water, I stood outside the tent and marveled at the total silence that surrounded us. Nothing moved, not even the ice beneath our feet.

At least the roar of the wind had left us, but this yearned-for silence wasn't quite what I had in mind. Soon the tent and two sleds were covered in a soft blanket of snow. I was surprised when Charlie left the comfort of the tent to stand close at my side as though experiencing the same silence and isolation I felt. I wondered if he felt as isolated from the rest of the world as I did.

My mouth had developed a cotton-like dryness. My throat felt dry and raspy and swallowing had become painful. The urgent need for more water dominated my thoughts. I had already calculated that I should reach the aircraft's pickup destination in three days, but now I worried that my increasing hunger and thirst might defeat me. This journey had been whittled down to the level of pure survival. My head throbbed and waves of nausea swept my body. My hands were healing and most of the pain had gone, but thirst had become a driving force on this desperate march to reach our pickup point and then on to all the water I could drink. I patted Charlie's head. He was still strong and showed no signs of distress. Half rations and eating ice appeared to be all he needed for now. My thoughts turned to Helena Island. Surely I should see it today.

By three in the morning the falling snow began to ease as the wind rose and the temperature dropped into the minus column. When visibility increased to one hundred feet I decided to leave. The weather was unsettled, but my frustration over the constant delays had become unbearable. I was encouraged to find that the lack of a strong headwind enabled me to travel at a much faster pace. A mile later amid a rising wind, my ever-increasing weakness from hunger and thirst slowed my pace, and no matter how hard I tried to ignore it, my skis moved slower than they had the previous day. At ten o'clock we were headed into a howling headwind that had become a sheer torment, lashing my face and body without mercy. The unceasing wind, combined with a savage hunger and thirst, made me dig deep into a reservoir of strength, discipline, and the absolute desire to continue. I dug so deep I found reserves I never knew I had to push my weakening body forward. I simply had to finish the journey. The end was so near. Once more, I encouraged Charlie to walk behind me so that he could take advantage of the shelter my body provided. He quickly got the idea and walked right on my heels. By now the lack of food and water made it increasingly difficult to keep warm. My caloric intake just wasn't sufficient to maintain inner body warmth. Whenever I stopped, I immediately began to shiver, and then it took at least an hour of hard skiing to regain warmth. In such a wind it was better to continue steadily onward, stopping only to quickly grab a chunk of chopped ice from the top of my sled, pass a piece to an expectant Charlie, and press on, head down, trying to make the best of a bad day. Eating ice caused my body to feel even colder, but I was desperate for fluid. When I felt severe stomach cramps, though, I realized that I had to stop eating ice. I gave the last piece to Charlie.

The sun shone through white streaks of clouds that sped across the sky. All too frequently the distant high-pitched scream of an incoming powerful gust signaled yet another blast that ripped across the ice, often sending me scrambling to stay upright. Although deep into survival mode, I fought through the wind. My wind-battered body was winning the battle. With every mile the journey's end drew closer.

Never once did Charlie waver or complain. He walked along, head down, following behind in his sheltered spot. Once more, I wondered what he must be thinking of all this. Under these conditions he normally would have been curled up on the ice, his back to the wind, sleeping through the storm. To walk through such a storm would have made no sense in his doggy world. Hour by hour we struggled on. I soon lost track of time as I forced my way ahead to the steady roar of the wind, concentrating on the rhythm of my skis sliding forward with each step. Even as my protesting body slowed with fatigue, I was so engrossed in making forward progress that I no longer paused to take even an occasional rest break.

After eighteen brutal hours and nineteen hard-won miles, I stopped for the day. The cutting, frigid wind was too strong to erect the tent, so I once again took refuge in my sled for a few hours of rest. First, I fed Charlie, who then curled up on the sheltered side of my sled and fell fast asleep. I ate my last two walnuts, drank my last sip of water for the day, and climbed into the sled, pulling my sleeping bag around me. The sled rocked as the gusts slammed into its side, but I was safe from the wind inside the zipped-up bag. We were only eight miles from Helena. In spite of the weather and my deteriorating body, I felt encouraged. If the storm cleared at least a little, Charlie and I should soon see the high northern cliffs of the island.

When I awoke at five A.M. it took me a few moments to realize that a deep silence had replaced the howl of the wind. The silence seemed unnatural. At last the storm had passed by. Excited to get going again, I hurriedly climbed out of the sled. My excitement was dashed when I saw that we were engulfed in a gray fog so thick that not a single ray of sunshine peeked through. I couldn't even see the length of the sled. I yelled in frustration, "When is this blasted junk going to stop?" Not surprisingly, no one answered. Charlie didn't even raise his head.

It seemed that everything was being thrown in my path to prevent me from reaching the finish point of this expedition. I was beyond exasperated! We were so close. All we needed was a break in the weather. Charlie seemed not to notice the fog and my frustration, or perhaps he had already figured out that the fog had us pinned down for at least awhile, so he might as well enjoy some extra sleep.

Now that the wind had calmed, at least I could put the tent up and have more room to rest. I would wait to depart until I could see a reasonable distance ahead. I still couldn't see Helena. As soon as the tent was erected, Charlie rose and without so much as an invitation he headed inside to take up a comfortable position on my already laid-out sleeping bag.

I was desperate to ski onward, but dared not because in the last few miles I had noticed a few wide cracks in the ice. Although easy to step across, they indicated that there might be areas where, with little visibility, I could drop into the water. My world was reduced to a featureless, gray, single dimension, where it was impossible to judge either scale or distance. At least my frustration at the weather took my mind off my growing hunger and thirst.

I lit the stove and melted enough ice to produce one pint of water to ration with the five walnuts during the day. For breakfast I allowed myself two walnuts, which I chewed a long time, then drank two sips of water.

At seven A.M. I looked out and whooped with joy. The fog had thinned and visibility, although still flat and providing negligible snow surface contrast, had vastly improved to about a quarter mile. It was safe to leave. I packed in record time, and with Charlie in his customary place at my side, we headed off to long-sought Helena Island and the end of our long journey. I soon discovered that no matter how hard I tried to disregard my growing weakness my pace had slowed. Charlie was not impressed with our speed. He was his usual energetic self. For the first hundred yards or so he kept looking up at me, as if waiting for me to take his hint to go faster. I patted his head and explained that this was all I could manage. As though irritated, he resorted to a few sharp barks to urge me onward. After getting no response, he seemed to resign himself to the situation and settled down to walk at my pace. This was my sixth day of low rations, and a serious weakness had set in. Throbbing headaches were an increasing problem as my body craved any sort of sustenance. I paced myself and made frequent stops to spread what energy I had left to cover the miles ahead. But we were getting there. I wearily plodded on, determined to make it.

As we started across an area of cement-hard ice ridges just inches high, a layer of ice fog only two feet thick rolled in to cover the surface for as far ahead as I could see. With no visible contrast or ability to see the ridges beneath my feet, I stumbled blindly onward, trying to keep my skis traveling in a straight line. I felt as if I was pushing my skis through a two-foot-thick layer of milk. But I was no match for the invisible ridges, which sent my skis slipping and twisting all over the place. I slowed down to regain some measure of control and at the same time avoid a collision with Charlie's paws. Now and then he jumped nimbly to one side to avoid my flying skis. Several hours later, around noon, weak shafts of golden sunlight forced their way through the clouds. As the blank whiteness around me brightened, the surface fog thinned enough to give me a better view of my footing and a more reasonable chance to stay upright. At least I wasn't traveling blind anymore. The improved conditions raised my spirits, and I even managed a little more speed, which seemed to make Charlie happy, judging by the spring in his step and his tail that waved back and forth.

As the fog thinned, I looked ahead and at last saw the glorious steep northern cliffs of Helena Island bathed in sunlight. At last I could see the very end of our journey. Nothing would stop us now, even if I had to crawl. My navigational calculations showed that I had already traveled 331 miles, and I had no more than thirty miles to go to reach our aircraft pickup point. "Look, Charlie, the cliffs! We're almost there," I said. If he understood my excitement, he gave no sign.

Mercifully, the wind stayed away as I veered farther east toward Cape Halkett on the eastern tip of Helena Island. From there my plan was to travel east across the three-mile stretch of ice to the Hosken Islands, a group of three islands joined to Sherard Osborn, the island where I'd begun the long journey throughout the magnetic North Pole region. After setting foot on the nearest of the Hosken Islands, I would then return to Helena, so that my triangular route through the entire Pole area would be complete.

The streaky, wind-torn clouds changed to an umbrella of solid gray and it began snowing lightly. Tiny flakes floated gently on a zigzag path down to land silently on the ice. Helena Island disappeared behind a curtain of flakes as I skied in the general direction of Cape Halkett.

The afternoon turned into evening as we toiled forward. We crossed two sets of fresh polar bear tracks that appeared to head west. For the last hour Charlie had frequently raised his nose to test the air for any scent drifting in on the air currents. I had hoped he smelled seals, but now realized that it had been bears that had remained unseen behind the curtain of heavy fog that had rolled in, reducing visibility once more to a few yards. Making matters worse, the ice around us began to move because of the swift currents that flowed between the islands. I jumped in fright at the sound of sharp rifle-like cracks and even louder explosions as the ice came alive. Narrow cracks in the ice shot past our feet. Charlie was even more disturbed than I was. I wanted to stop and camp, but dared not in such an unstable area. In another hour all seemed quieter and the ice was still. According to my navigation, Charlie and I were standing off the coast of Hosken Island, and its five-hundred-foot-high twin peaks. There was no chance of seeing them in the heavy fog, so I would have to wait to confirm our position.

I decided to put the tent up, and after hours of anxious waiting, around eleven o'clock it stopped snowing and the fog lifted just enough to allow me to see the twin peaks. I was so relieved I shouted with sheer joy to Charlie, "There they are. We're right on target!" He awoke with a start and jumped to his feet in alarm. I patted him and pointed to the peaks.

My excitement at having navigated all the way with no mistakes gave my thirsty, hungry body a new charge of energy. "We're almost home, Charlie," I said, giving him a celebratory hug. Although he might not have understood the reason for my whoops of joy, his waving tail told me that at least he appreciated the big hug I gave him.

The fog melted away, leaving everything bathed in sunlight. After a sip of water and two walnuts, plus a cup of dog food for Charlie, I broke camp at noon and headed toward Hoskens. In a short time, I stood on the island's shore about four hundred yards across from the unnamed twin peaks, their steep, white-streaked slopes glistening in the sunshine, standing side by side like two guards watching over a lonely, silent world. I turned my back on the peaks to look for the nearest smooth ice close to Helena for a landing strip.

But as I skied toward Helena, I realized I would have to find a landing strip somewhere on the southern coast of the island. The ice had been too rough along the entire northern coast. Now I could see that it was even rougher in the channel between Hosken and Helena, where the currents play havoc with the ice, turning it into a boulder alley.

We angled straight down the southeast coast, and after four miles I found solid smooth ice, perfect for an aircraft to land on. I camped about two hundred yards off the coast across from a deep, well-defined, frozen river-mouth that could easily be seen from the air. I called the charter service and base camp to give them my position coordinates and a description of my location.

Now Charlie and I stood within the southern boundary of the magnetic North Pole region for 1988. I was delighted, and also relieved that at last I didn't have to think about navigation and making good mileage. I could think about going back to base and the long-dreamed-of water and food.

Before I began the expedition, Bezal and Ruddi of Bradley Air Services and I had chosen Helena Island as the logical pickup point because it completed the triangular route I intended to travel throughout the Pole area and might enable a tourist plane to pick us up. When I called base, Ruddi told me that a tourist plane was to fly from Resolute to the Polaris Mine the next day, and while the tourists stayed there, the plane would fly north and pick Charlie and me up. Later, the tourists told me that they had asked to be the first people to greet me upon my return. Ruddi told me to radio him at nine o'clock the next morning to give him weather information. Weather permitting, two pilots hoped to arrive at my location about one o'clock the next afternoon.

As I put the tent up, it struck me that this would be my last camp. I shouted to the heavens, "No more camps, thank you, thank you!" It was almost beyond belief that we were actually going home to food and water and a real bed. After spending so long alone and consumed with navigation, traveling across uncertain ice, enduring storms, surviving on minimal food and water, and of course evading our neighbors the polar bears, it seemed almost unreal and hard to grasp.

While I erected the tent, Charlie raised his nose to test the air currents for bear or seal scent. Suddenly, in long bounding strides, he dashed toward the island to gleefully follow fresh bear tracks. "No, Charlie," I shouted. "Leave them alone." But he was on a mission, and with his nose pressed to the tracks, he raced off to find the bear. I dropped the tent anchor pegs and again, even louder, I shouted to him, "Come here!" He stopped and looked back at me, clearly disappointed. Again, but with even more urgency, I shouted, "Come here now!" He hesitated, torn between the possibility of finding the bear or returning to me. Walking toward him, I shouted again. With reluctance he slowly made his way to my side, stopping now and then to look longingly back at the tracks, which were only a couple of hours old. We still had to remain vigilant, although he apparently thought differently. Judging by the tracks, we had just missed another bear. I attached him to his lead to avoid any more episodes. Judging by the forlorn look he gave me, in his opinion I had once again failed in the area of sportsmanship.

I melted ice for my thermos to be ready for the morning. I left a half-cup of fuel in the fuel bottle, enough to melt ice for one more pint, just in case the weather turned worse and the plane couldn't fly tomorrow. I couldn't throw caution to the winds just yet. I still had to plan for emergencies. I ate my last two walnuts for the day, then climbed into my sleeping bag. But after only two hours, thirst woke me and I tossed and turned. I went out to check on Charlie. As I approached, he stood up and stretched. We had been going to bed late and getting up early for so long, and sleeping so little, that Charlie probably thought we were about to head out again. Since he was up, I invited him into the tent, but this time I led him in behind me so that I got to the sleeping bag first.

Charlie - The Hero by My Side

Representing two countries: USA and New Zealand. We celebrate our victorious but lonely arrival at the central coordinates of the magnetic North Pole.

Scanning for bears

Chapter Twelve —
The End in Sight

At last, at two A.M. on the twenty-seventh and final day of our journey, the wind had changed direction and the weather cleared. I couldn't sleep, so I ate the last handful of walnuts and drank half of the water for breakfast. By now the pain of swallowing even small sips was almost impossible to bear. Charlie ate his full day's ration, which left him one extra day's food in case the plane didn't reach us.

Before leaving the Pole area, I had only one more task to complete. I wanted to climb the cliffs of Helena and stand on its high plateau. Just as I had been fascinated with the prospect of walking on King Christian Island at the northern edge of the magnetic Pole region, I had dreamed of standing on Helena Island on the Pole's southern edge, but especially atop the high cliffs of Helena, an island only twenty-five miles long by eight miles wide. Although my energy level had hit rock bottom, I was determined to complete the expedition as planned. All my life I had been a goal-setter, a planner, and a finisher. I knew that even in my weakened state I had to at least do my best to achieve this one last piece of the journey. I stuffed a few necessary items into my backpack and, with my flare gun in my pocket and the loaded rifle slung over my shoulder, Charlie and I set off toward Helena in the early morning light. We hiked up a frozen shallow ravine and then attacked the steep, high cliffs. I climbed slowly with frequent stops to avoid waves of nausea. Charlie, whose home had always been at sea level, had never climbed such a steep, high place before. At first, he seemed unsure of how to attack the steep angle and clawed his way up, staying close at my side as I encouraged him. Halfway up he found his confidence and eagerly led the way to the top. Although hunger and thirst made me feel as if I had just climbed a twenty-thousand-foot mountain, it was worth every step. Helena was as rugged and steep as King Christian had been flat and gentle. The wind stripped naked its high cliffs and plateaus, and rocks were strewn about, covered in lichen that existed in defiance of the violence it endured. It was all a contrast to the grayish gravel and ice-covered gentle slopes of King Christian, which blended almost unnoticed with the sea.

Together we crossed the five-hundred-foot-high plateau and walked northeast to stand on the high cliffs of the island. It sounded strange to hear the crunch of small rocks beneath my boots after almost a month on snow and ice. The islands all around me were splendid in the clear morning light. I looked north across the white blanket of sea ice toward King Christian Island, invisible in the far distance. The windswept open sea ice we had traveled both north and south looked boundless and empty beneath the pale-blue canopy that arched above us. There was nothing in the immense icy vista that indicated that humans had ever been there. I reflected on the hardships we had experienced along the way and on what Charlie and I had accomplished.

And of course, there was my buddy Charlie standing at my side, his black fur ruffling in the cold wind. My gratitude toward him was infinite. Our bond of love and trust had grown daily. He had faithfully warned me of polar bears and had even saved my life. The only time he disagreed with my judgment was when his natural instinct and wisdom warned him for good reason to question my decision. I had learned that when he hesitated, it was time for me to take notice. Even during the many long hard days, he'd plodded along at my side without complaint. He taught me patience when faced with storms or conditions that made travel unsafe.

He was indeed the hero by my side. Now I looked forward to taking him home with me, introducing him to Bill, and showing him the ways of a world foreign to him.

We had been away over an hour. I had to be back at camp in time for the aircraft nine A.M. radio call. With surprising reluctance and sadness and one last long look north across the silent sweeping vista that Charlie and I had spent so many challenging days crossing, I headed down with Charlie close on my heels. As we climbed down to the sea ice, the thought occurred to me that perhaps I could return with Bill. I had a yearning to share with him this place that had become so special to me. We did indeed return four years later to ski, pulling our own sleds, again without dog teams, snowmobiles, or aircraft, to the magnetic North Pole. It was a journey of celebration of the thirtieth anniversary of a close-knit marriage and friendship.

Back at camp I set up the radio for the planned periodic calls to base camp to report weather conditions to the pilot who would pick us up at about one P.M.

Later, the aircraft call sign "Delta, November, Delta," came over the radio. They were on their way. Soon I spotted the plane in the far distance. It was with enormous relief that I told Charlie, "Now at last we don't have to watch for polar bears." I felt as if a ton of weight had been lifted from my shoulders. I'm not sure that Charlie would have agreed with me. After all, here we were right in the middle of polar bear habitat with abundant opportunities for a good polar bear chase.

Soon the Twin Otter aircraft landed on wide skis and taxied amid a cloud of blowing snow kicked up by the propeller. With huge grins the pilot and co-pilot jumped out, the first people I had seen in almost a month. I was excited to actually talk to people in person rather than by radio. After a boisterous greeting of hugs, backslaps, and congratulations, the pilot told me that most of the Arctic had been listening to my nightly radio calls. They told me that many had doubted that a woman alone on foot, without the support of a dog team or snowmobile, would survive the polar bears and the violent storms of an unusually turbulent spring.

"Well," I said, "Charlie was always there when I needed him. He was a real trooper all the way."

Paying special attention to Charlie, they hugged him and told him, "Good boy Charlie! You did a good job. You've become a famous dog. We all worried about you and those bears." Obviously agreeing with his new admirers, Charlie fanned his bushy tail back and forth.

Our plane arrives - time to go home

Daily struggle has ended…no more bears

Chapter Thirteen —
Our Triumphant Return

I took my tent down one last time while the pilots loaded Charlie's sled first and then mine. Although I was happy and relieved to have successfully finished the expedition, the day-after-day struggle to overcome all odds had been so intense that I felt that I was leaving a part of my inner self at the Pole. Now with Charlie, my hero and constant faithful companion, we were going home. Together we were about to start a new expedition. Charlie was no longer regarded as just another dog, but was now elevated to the status of hero. He was invited to board the aircraft first and given a window seat with a jacket spread out to protect him from the cold surface of the metal seat.

As we flew back over the ice to the Polaris Mine, I strained to see any sign of our tracks or even a campsite, but of course there was none. The wind had swept all away as if we had never been there. Perhaps it was better that way. After all, we had been merely visitors passing through. But if no sign of our journey remained, the awesome presence of the Arctic would never leave my memory. Now Charlie and I, after 364 miles and twenty-seven days, were going home.

At the Polaris Mine a large group of tourists who had been staying at Resolute had learned from Bezal and Terry of Charlie's and my journey to the Pole. They had listened to my nightly radio calls and followed our daily progress. Now they were visiting Polaris and had waited there to be the first to greet Charlie and me. It was an enthusiastic welcome. Charlie eagerly basked in the attention of the twenty-three enthusiasts, who crowded around to greet us and stroke his broad back. To them, just as he had been to the pilots, Charlie was the hero of the moment. I stood by while he absorbed all the attention and the many tasty morsels he was offered by his eager admirers. I felt like a proud mother whose child had just received the ultimate in respect and recognition.

After almost a month alone it was somewhat overwhelming to suddenly be surrounded by laughing, talking, enthusiastic people. However, Charlie was the star and he knew it. I stood back to watch the spectacle as it unfolded. Not only did he greet each person with a soft touch of his muzzle, but then he really entered into the joyful atmosphere by laying on his back and pedaling his legs to invite a tummy scratch. He was indisputably brilliant in his new career as a tourist attraction. He accepted any and all treats, and of course looked for more. Everyone fell in love with him and all would have liked to take him home. I had no doubt that this dynamic bundle of energy who could charge a polar bear with the aggression of a charging buffalo would be a mellow attraction with everyone back home.

We stayed overnight at Polaris. Charlie was escorted to the same equipment shed he had slept in before our journey. He was fed a luxurious meal of caribou meat, and I was assured that he would be safe and comfortable until morning. After being shown to my room I hurried to the dining room, which was always open during the day. My first desire was to quench my thirst. Although my throat hurt to swallow, I drank from the lemonade machine until I could drink no more. Next, I ate my fill of sandwiches and pie. At last, my energy had returned to a tolerable level. Then I called Bill. "Congratulations, you made it!" He cheered. He'd already called Mother and Dad. "They're both relieved you're okay and coming home," he said. "I called them every week so they could keep up with your progress. They don't expect you to call them until you get home." Home! What a wonderful thought that was. I went to sleep that night in a real bed in a building with a real roof over my head, with no worries about weather or polar bears. I slept soundly all night.

The next day Charlie and I said goodbye to our new friends at Polaris who had gone out of their way to extend hospitality and kindness both before and after the expedition. We prepared to leave for the short fifty-seven-mile flight to Resolute to continue our journey homeward. We were the first ones on the plane and quickly settled into the two front seats that had been reserved for us. At our next stop, our base camp at Resolute, we received another boisterous welcome from the local Inuit, who treated Charlie with attention not normally given to local dogs. He had proven his considerable skill when dealing with polar bears, and in the Inuit culture that was more than enough to elevate him to a special status.

The next six days spent at Resolute, while we waited for the commercial aircraft to take us south, were filled with the confusion of adjusting to what society considers a normal, civilized way of life. Sitting at a dinner table with others seemed strange that first evening. Forgotten table manners suddenly became important, although sharing space with fellow humans was definitely easier than coexisting with polar bears. The long-awaited shower was almost a disaster. I had so often looked forward to the joys of hot water cascading over my body. But the sudden warmth, to which I was now unaccustomed, almost made me pass out. I quickly adjusted the faucet to lukewarm. A distant barking dog, which in former times I would not have noticed, was now a constant annoyance as I adjusted to the sounds of habitation. Dogs were not welcome indoors, so I erected my tent and slept outdoors after that first night at the mine so that Charlie could sleep at my side until the time to leave Resolute. We had become so closely bonded that I hated to be away from him even to sleep.

On our last day in Resolute we were up before daybreak, eager to be on time at the airport to take the jet to Vancouver, British Columbia. I was told that Charlie required vaccination and rabies shots, the first of his life, before we could enter the United States. We had to first fly to Vancouver and then pick up my car, which I had left parked close to the airport, and drive to a veterinary clinic. A friend gave me the name of a clinic, and I called them from Resolute and informed them of our approximate time of arrival.

Leaving the Arctic was another day of adjustment as Charlie and I said goodbye to the uncomplicated life of Resolute and entered the world of hustle and bustle. Charlie faced a new life and new experiences. I worried that he might miss his old lifestyle, but I soon discovered his vast capacity to adjust. Even the airline staff had heard of Charlie's and my expedition to the Pole: they treated us like royalty. They reserved the two front seats for us and arranged to have special doggy treats and a water bowl available for Charlie during the hour-and-a-half flight. Normally dogs would have traveled in a kennel with the cargo, but they decided, much to my relief, that Charlie warranted special accommodations. When they put the seat belt around him, he sat back completely relaxed, as if he had traveled this way every day of his life.

After we arrived at the Vancouver airport, our first task was to find a bus that would take Charlie and me to the Car Park about a mile away. The first bus driver said, "No dogs on my bus!" and abruptly slammed the door. The next bus driver was more understanding. A dog lover, he liked Charlie on sight and allowed us to board, even giving us a front seat.

My car was a medium-sized Honda Civic with limited space available for my expedition gear and a large dog. It had been a challenge to find space for everything in March when I had driven to the airport before the expedition, but now I had to find room for Charlie, who had never ridden in a car in his life. He eagerly jumped onto the front seat and seemed happy there, but I felt compelled to find more space for him in the back. After some innovative rearranging of the load, there was just enough room on one side. Charlie, although reluctant to leave the front seat, finally agreed to settle down in the back.

The next hurdle was to find the clinic. An hour later, after several wrong turns that I hadn't taken in the Arctic, we arrived. As we walked in, I was surprised to see a local constable at the door, complete with shotgun. His only response to my greeting was a slight nod of his head while he kept his eyes fixed on Charlie. *There must be an emergency of some sort,* I thought. And when Charlie stepped forward in his usual friendly tail-wagging way to greet people, everyone stepped back as if he might attack. *Surely they don't think he's a wild animal I found in the Arctic?* When he approached the receptionist, she panicked and dashed to safety behind her counter. But Charlie was not to be fazed by such odd behavior. He merely yawned and sat down as if prepared to stay the day. I felt the tension leave the room as everyone gave a collective sigh of relief and frowns turned to smiles. It turned out that when I had phoned the clinic from Resolute and told them that Charlie was a polar bear dog, the staff had immediately become fearful of how such a dog might react to strangers. Now that Charlie was the center of attention, he really turned on the charm. He rolled on his back to invite the usual tummy scratch. With a laugh the constable stepped forward and obliged with a vigorous belly rub. Then, stepping over to the counter, he reached into a jar and took out a couple of doggy treats. Charlie immediately jumped to his feet. Food was far more important than even a good belly rub, and he took each piece gently. The good-humored constable was still laughing as he turned to leave. "Well, my civic duty is done for the day. I can leave now that this vicious, dangerous dog is under control."

But even I held my breath as they produced the vaccination needle and proceeded to part his fur and push the needle through his skin. I expected at least a yelp or a flinch. I relaxed and breathed again when there was no reaction. Apparently, all the attention and treats made a jab with a sharp needle worthwhile.

After he received all of his required vaccinations, I took Charlie outside and tied him to a tree so that he could relieve himself. After I paid the bill, I left to rejoin Charlie but gasped in horror as I took in his version of landscaping. He had dug up the surrounding beauty bark with his huge front paws, which had acted like backhoes. Beauty bark, soil, and vegetation had flown in all directions, covering the lawn and path. Somewhat sheepishly, I went back inside to ask for a broom. Thankfully, they all thought it was hilarious and helped me clean up the mess. But then we had afresh challenge. Just as soon as we replaced the soil and the bark to its rightful place, Charlie seemed to think it was some sort of game and sent it all flying again. The only solution was to take him inside, away from temptation. Finally, with everyone's help, everything was back in place. The only casualties were a couple of plants that were shredded and well beyond saving. Now we could continue on our way home. I found Charlie dozing on the waiting room couch without a care in the world, totally oblivious to the fact that the entire staff and I had spent an hour cleaning up his mess. After some persuasion and more treats, he agreed to leave the couch and I led him to the car, where a new problem presented itself. He insisted on sitting in the front seat. It seemed that the space in the back wasn't to his liking. After thirty minutes of reloading, I cleared the seat and Charlie climbed in. Although his copious frame overflowed the seat, he seemed contented with the arrangement, so we left for the Canadian border. The border official looked at my passport and Charlie's vaccination papers, and like a proud mother I expected some praise for the very large black dog at my side. To my intense disappointment the official never even looked at Charlie, and I drove away wondering how anyone could ignore my handsome companion.

Our first stop was an Interstate 5 rest area. Now that Charlie was in a new country, I thought he might like to look around the park-like setting before continuing on to his new home. He decided to use a large alder tree as a relief post. But he was unaccustomed to trees and it took some serious adjustment to stand just right and aim the urine stream to land on the base of the tree trunk. Once having completed the most basic of tasks, it was time to examine a large clump of yellow dandelions. He thrust his black nose deep into the flowers and immediately pulled back with a sneeze that shook his entire body. He had never sniffed pollen before, and it irritated his nose. He had barely recovered from his encounter with flower pollen when he spied a gray squirrel. He made a leaping dive toward to the furry animal. But he was no match for the squirrel, which dashed for a tree and scampered up into the branches, well out of reach of a determined Charlie, who frantically reached up the tree trunk, trying to grab his quarry. Then, to add insult to injury, the squirrel sat barely out of reach, chattering loudly, teasing a frustrated Charlie. Thinking that he deserved a treat after so much activity, I went to the car to get some bite-size treats that the veterinarian had given me. With treats in hand, I turned back to Charlie. *"Oh no, not again!"* Head down, tail up, he was completely engrossed in digging a large hole in the lawn. This was government grass, and I could just imagine the trouble we might find ourselves in. I grabbed his collar, dashed back to the car, and without ceremony shoved Charlie in and drove away, glad that we had not been seen. So far this had been anything but a dull day.

Because of Bill's professional flying schedule he had been unable to meet us earlier and had arranged an afternoon flight to Seattle. Due to Charlie's various escapades, we were running late, but I still took time to stop at a pet store to buy him a new matching black collar and lead.

Charlie in his beloved Cascade mountains

The kids loved Charlie

Chapter Fourteen —
Home

I was so excited to have Bill meet our new addition to the family that I couldn't sit while we waited for his flight. We strolled around the baggage claim area, which was in a state of pandemonium as various flights arrived and people anxiously dashed around looking for luggage. I was concerned that Charlie might become uncomfortable amid the unaccustomed commotion, but I need not have worried. Charlie was blessed with the gift of a calm nature. With endless charm he captivated the people around us, many of whom interrupted their search for an elusive piece of luggage to pat him and tell me, "What a beautiful dog."

Eventually Bill arrived. After we embraced, Bill, looking surprised as he hugged Charlie, exclaimed, "So this is Charlie. He's a lot bigger than I imagined. We owe you a lot, boy." Charlie responded with his usual enthusiastic tail wagging and licked Bill's hand. Taking Charlie's lead, Bill led us out to the car and we set out for Charlie's new home. Two hours later we drove up the long steep driveway of our twelve-acre property in the foothills of Washington state's Cascade Mountains.

Charlie had never seen a cat, and I knew that our seventeen-pound black tomcat would be the first of our animal family to greet us. While Bill unloaded the car, I gingerly invited Charlie inside the kitchen to meet Tom. At the unexpected sight of a canine stranger, the cat immediately arched his back, paused a moment, then marched straight up to Charlie and, with claws out, took a solid swipe at Charlie's nose. A surprised Charlie reared back. I instantly stepped between the two, dreading Charlie's response to such impolite treatment. To my total surprise, Charlie, after he regained his composure and licked a drop of blood off his nose, wiggled up to Tom as if begging for the cat's friendship. Tom merely looked at him with haughty disdain, turned his back, and arrogantly walked away. Rising to his feet, Charlie followed Tom into the living room where the cat, with a sudden change of heart, turned and rubbed his back on Charlie's nose and purred. I couldn't believe my eyes. With one pounce and a crunch Charlie could have easily killed Tom, but instead he had just made his first friend—so much so that from then on, they frequently slept side by side.

Next stop was the dog field, where our three other dogs spent their daytime hours romping and playing. They all rushed up to greet the newcomer. It was immediately noticeable that although Charlie was the new dog on the block, no one was willing to challenge him and everyone seemed content to elevate him to the alpha position. Charlie clearly demanded the role as alpha and with tail held high he proudly went through the ritual of circling and sniffing each of his new companions. Once his inspection was over, he began the scrutiny of the field. With an entourage of all three dogs following him, he walked the perimeter of the two-acre field and then, apparently satisfied with his new accommodations, proceeded to dig a hole in one corner. This time I made no move to stop him. This was the dog field, and he could dig to his heart's content. With enthusiasm he concentrated on the task at hand. I left to help Bill unload the car, and when I returned an hour later the hole was at least three feet deep and Charlie's three companions had gleefully joined in the project. They all loved to dig, and Charlie's formidable skill as an earth excavator had met with absolute approval.

Our ten goats had still not met Charlie. It took some time to persuade him to leave his digging project, but once he saw the goats, he thought the interruption was well worth it. One goat—named Snowy—was a large, pure white Saanen breed. Ignoring the rest of the goats, Charlie fixed his undivided attention on Snowy. At first all went well as Charlie followed the goat and sniffed his long white fur, seemingly curious about this animal that was the color of the more familiar polar bear but was much smaller and smelled a lot different. After thirty minutes or so, Charlie decided that he should investigate the longer fur on Snowy's flanks. A couple of sharp tugs convinced Snowy that this was just going too far. Uttering a high-pitched bleat that screamed *Help!* he raced away to escape the pesky dog.

That was all Charlie needed. He sprinted after Snowy and grabbed him by his rear leg, just as I had watched him grab a polar bear. A terrified Snowy was thrown to the ground as his operatic voice rose to a panicked shriek for help. I dashed into the fray to separate them and grabbed Charlie's collar. After considerable tugging and pulling, I finally dragged him back to rejoin his canine companions in the dog field. From then on, a secure fence separated Charlie from the goats. But Snowy continued to fascinate Charlie. Soon, Snowy appeared to have forgiven Charlie's transgression, and they often spent hours pressed up against the fence, visiting. Charlie ignored the rest of the goat herd and we figured that was because Snowy was the only pure white goat in the herd of ten. Perhaps it was the color that counted most in Charlie's world.

At first Charlie didn't bark, but he sometimes howled or made yipping sounds like a wolf. This didn't surprise me, as I had noticed Charlie's lack of a genuine dog-like bark on our journey to the Pole. Our other dogs would turn their heads from side to side listening, puzzled by Charlie's seemingly odd version of barking. It was a couple of months before Charlie copied them and developed a dog-like bark that was loud and forceful.

The local community celebrated Charlie's and my return with a celebration of around five hundred people. Bill and I were concerned that the large crowd might be overwhelming for Charlie, because this would be yet another new experience. Our concern was unfounded. He quickly became the center of attention and unashamedly basked in his newfound fame. There was no limit to his capacity to win human hearts.

We were eager to introduce Charlie to our favorite mountain trails in the Cascades. By now one of Charlie's favorite pastimes was riding in the car. He loved to press his nose close to the front window as if piloting us onward. The problem was that he demanded the front passenger seat as his own. Without success we tried to persuade him that his place was on the back seat. Clearly taken aback by our demands, he ignored us—and with a look of impetuous resolution he settled his large frame on the front seat as if it was to be a permanent arrangement. To be exiled to the back seat was, in his judgment, a total disregard for his comfort. Bill and I agreed to a compromise. The two front seats were separated by a space wide enough for Charlie to stand between us and attend to his piloting duties. We were certain that he enjoyed his triumph.

We resumed our usual routine of mountain hiking two days a week. Charlie loved the trails, especially the higher snow-covered ones. He gleefully rolled in the snow, and after indulging in a luxurious icy back scratch, he gulped large mouthfuls of snow. Only then would he agree to proceed. His ability to adapt to the warmer climate of Washington state was of concern to us, especially in the warmer mid-summer months. During those months we were careful to hike the more shaded trails that provided a cooler journey for Charlie, and although he eventually drank from the mountain streams, we always carried his own quart bottle of water. In the beginning we were puzzled that even on a hot day he refused to step off the trail to drink from a nearby stream. Then we realized that he had been trained, as a member of an Inuit sled-pulling team, that no dog should dare step off the trail without permission. It took a few hikes to teach him that he could drink whenever he wanted.

On our first overnight camping trip with Charlie we invited our friend Margaret with us. Our gear was loaded into the covered back of her pickup truck. Margaret drove and Bill sat in the front seat. Charlie and I sat in the two back seats. We had not traveled more than a mile when Charlie decided that his rightful place was in the front passenger seat. "Charlie, you stay back here with me," I said as I grabbed his collar and pulled him back. With a sad look in my direction, he reluctantly obeyed. Moments later he pawed at the side window. This was a signal that he wanted to put his head out the open window, apparently to enjoy the feeling of air rushing past his face. When it proved too much he would retreat. Now his raised paw told me to open the window. He not only leaned with his head out, but also draped both front paws over the windowsill with half his body dangling over the vehicle's side and his nose pressed into the rushing air. Although we were moving pretty slowly on that rough, gravel mountain road, it wasn't a good idea for our dog to be hanging halfway out of the vehicle. I pulled him by his collar and reached over to close the window to prevent further adventures. Not to be outdone, with his mind still set on the front seat, he tried again to push forward. Bill, tired of the wrestling match going on in the back seat, said with a firm edge to his voice, "For heaven's sake, Charlie, here, take my seat!" Margaret stopped while Bill and Charlie changed seats.

Now Charlie's black head and half his ninety-four-pound body completely obscured the driver to anyone looking in from the right-hand side. It appeared that a large black dog was driving. I will never forget a lady's look of amazement when we stopped to read a roadside historical sign. Obviously a tourist, she stood transfixed when she saw this big black dog arrive driving a truck. Speechless, she frantically beckoned her male companion to look. He turned and stared with an expression of disbelief. Having decided that we were attracting too much attention, the normally unflappable Margaret promptly drove off, muttering, "People just don't get it. Has the woman never seen a dog before?" Bill and I had suffered through this reaction many times, and although not surprised, we were happy to drive away without the need to explain our canine's driving habits. Now that Charlie was happily guiding us onward to distant horizons, we proceeded without further incident.

Although Charlie was used to sleeping on nothing but snow and ice in the Arctic, we wanted to provide every comfort for him, so on overnight camping trips we carried his sleeping pad. We soon discovered that Charlie was not content to sleep on his foam pad. Instead, as soon as the tent was erected, he immediately dashed into the tent to claim my sleeping bag. It was easier to give in to him, so I usually ended up sleeping on his pad while he slept the night away spread out on mine. It definitely brought back memories of our sleeping arrangement on our way to the Pole.

We always kept him on a long lead, mindful of the fact that he would chase after any wild animal that we might encounter. Although it was great sport for him, we realized that he could be lost in the mountains just as many other unleashed dogs had been over the years. One evening just as the golden light began to fade over the surrounding mountaintops, the scent of a passing coyote on the far bank of the shallow stream we camped alongside drifted in over the gentle breeze. Somehow the clasp on Charlie's lead came unclipped. In an instant he jetted across the water after the coyote. The coyote, with one startled look, raced away from the black tyrant. As they sprinted across an open space, Charlie reached the coyote just as it was about to leap over a steep ravine. We yelled at the top of our voices for Charlie to stop. Did he hear us? Or did he decide that the chase over the ravine wasn't worth it? With a last snap at the coyote's tail, Charlie stopped and, with an aura of triumph, returned with a trophy of coyote fur in his jaws.

On one hike into a high-altitude mountain lake, the route traversed a steep slope covered in small rocks that provided unstable footing. A fall would have resulted in a two-hundred-foot plunge with uncertain results. It was Bill's turn to take Charlie's lead, but just as we were about to start downward Charlie stopped and refused to go ahead. Bill suggested I take Charlie's lead. The moment I did so, Charlie confidently stepped out in front to take me down the unstable slope. Even though he had formed a strong bond with Bill, it was my safety that he was most concerned with. This was one of many times that Charlie would act as my guide and make sure I was safe. Just as he had on the expedition to the Pole, Charlie—even now, in a much safer environment—wanted to protect me from harm.

We hiked hundreds of mountain trails. He could never get enough hikes. Once when we hiked one of his favorite trails to a high mountain lake, we came to a fork in the trail. Bill and I were sure that we should take the left-hand fork, but Charlie made it clear that we should follow him on the right-hand fork. He was so determined that we decided to follow him although it was against our better judgment. We were somewhat embarrassed to discover that he was right. He knew the way better than we did.

One of our favorite journeys was a three-hundred-mile hike on the Pacific Crest Trail through Washington state to Canada. Charlie learned to recognize the various trailheads. As soon as we arrived at a trailhead, he made it known that it was time to get started. When we stopped on the trail for a water or food break, he set a definite time limit. When time was up, he barked to urge us to get going again. He never followed, but instead walked ahead, leading us at a brisk pace. He was convinced that his role was that of a leader, not a follower. His alpha personality meant that any dog we might meet on a trail was in his opinion a trespasser. When such meetings occurred, his whole attitude radiated outrage. With bared teeth and loud snarls, he not only reduced most dogs we met to whimpering shadows of themselves, he also caused their owners to grab the dogs and flee the noisy onslaught with our shouts of apology echoing in their ears. To avoid such confrontations, at the first sign of an approaching dog, Bill would step in front of Charlie while I shortened his lead and tucked in close behind as we hurried past. Once past, Charlie acted as if nothing out of the ordinary had happened. By contrast, these confrontations left Bill and me with deeply etched memories.

On the other hand, people were most welcome on Charlie's trails. As they passed, he would step toward them, expecting at least a pat, which he usually received. If a hiker passed without giving Charlie what in his mind was the required attention, he would stare after them as they disappeared along the trail as if wondering how someone could ever ignore him.

A favorite activity that became an almost daily ritual when we weren't hiking was for Charlie to accompany Bill and me on our cross-country skiing or our daily run. Our runs took place on the local golf course. All of the groundskeepers-men knew of Charlie's past and our journey to the Pole. They often met us with treats and soon became Charlie's friends. One day a man in the midst of mowing the grass stopped nearby and momentarily left his machine. Unfortunately, he left his lunch within easy reach. Charlie was used to visiting the workers, so he trotted over to greet his friend. Then he spied the lunch bag. In a flash he consumed the sandwich, paper bag and all, then had the gall to wait for his friend to give him the usual pat. We were appalled and embarrassed, but fortunately the now lunch-less man thought it hilarious and even an honor that this famous and gentle dog had eaten his lunch. We later heard stories that were circulated far and wide, some greatly exaggerated, about how Charlie stole the lunch, bag and all.

Our small farm was home to the dogs and goats I've already mentioned, but also cats, chickens, and one donkey. Donkeys are fussy animals and like to choose a place in the field to claim as their bathroom, producing a pile of manure. Quite some time went by, perhaps a year, before Charlie took any interest in donkey manure. But, being a dog, one morning Charlie decided that a nice roll in the stuff would improve his day. Then he approached us in the garden. His odor was powerful and totally unsuitable for a dog whose residence included the house. A bath was the solution. The problem was that Charlie had a strong aversion to water. He hated it! But the evil deed had to be accomplished somehow. From the barn we took a shallow trough and filled it with warm water. Charlie sensed what was about to happen and left in a hurry for the far field. We called him to return *now!* He of course suddenly developed acute deafness and ignored our calls. There was only one thing we could do: take his lead and bring him back to face a bath that was about to become a distressing ordeal for all involved. His physical strength and determination to avoid the water at all costs were beyond anything we had so far observed in his character. With considerable shoving and pushing we finally managed to force him into the tub, but not before all three of us were thoroughly wet from head to toe. Once in the tub, he at first sat with the gloomiest of looks, then attempted a dash for freedom. After an epic struggle that further drenched Bill and me, we returned him to the tub. While I held him down, Bill proceeded to spread shampoo from head to toe and scrub the awful stench from the thick coat.

Next came the rinse water. All the while Charlie's countenance screamed the deepest outrage that such indignity should be forced upon him. Finally, when he was reasonably clean and odor-free, we allowed him to leave the tub. As if in revenge, he gave a colossal shake, sending a shower of water to drench us once more. For the rest of the day he avoided us. But dinnertime turned events in our favor. An extra helping of treats added to his normal food did the trick. We were forgiven and once more all was well in Charlie's world. Perhaps he now understood the problem with odorous manure, because he never rolled in it again. We eventually solved the problem of bathing by taking him to a local groomer, who plied him with treats and copious helpings of attention. Charlie still detested the water but withstood the bathing procedure in good grace in return for the special attention that elevated him to movie star status.

As a public speaker I was invited to many schools to tell the story of Charlie's and my journey to the magnetic North Pole. Charlie quickly discovered that schools meant lots of kids who would swarm him with hugs and pats and even kisses. He loved it: so much attention, and it was all his. As soon as we arrived at a school, his tail would wave back and forth in anticipation of being the center of their undivided attention. He also accompanied me to hundreds of adult events where I was the speaker. At book signings people lined up not only to receive a signed book but to pat Charlie. It always amused Bill and me to see people flock to fuss over Charlie long before we were ever noticed. Even when I was a convention keynote speaker Charlie always took center stage.

Once we returned home, I set about writing a book about Charlie's and my trek to the Pole. I named the book Polar Dream. The journey had indeed been a dream that had come true. Of course, Charlie is the star of the story.

Simon & Schuster, the publishers, sent us both on a national tour. We appeared together on *Good Morning America* and the *Today* show and in several national publications, including *Reader's Digest*. The book soon became a national best seller, thanks in no small part to Charlie. Whether before television cameras or at my side in interviews, he was always a placid, unruffled presence, even when we flew long distances to large cities.

Our trip to New York was a near-disaster, though. The rules required Charlie to travel in a large dog crate in the plane's hold with the luggage. He hated it! I was a nervous wreck the whole way and drove the flight attendant to distraction with my constant inquiries about Charlie's safety. It took four long hours for our flight to arrive in New York. After disembarking I eagerly looked forward to greeting Charlie and then boarding the limousine that the publisher had provided to take us to our hotel. At first there was pandemonium while everyone searched for their bags. Then everyone left and still Charlie had not appeared. Now I was desperate. I asked at the Lost and Found desk if they had seen a large black dog. The hour was late and a weary, uninterested woman told me with an irritatingly dismissive wave of her hand that she had no idea where any dog was and promptly went back to rearranging a pile of papers. By now I was frantic with worry and outraged by her indifferent attitude. I tossed diplomacy aside and ordered, in my best drill sergeant voice, "Find him *now!*" My angry tone gained her immediate attention. She looked up, nervously rearranged her large, black-rimmed glasses, paused a moment, then fled to find a manager. Minutes later he scurried to the counter and, partly out of breath, offered apologies. Then, after a couple of phone calls, he told me that Charlie was on a plane ready to take off for Finland.

To say that I was upset would be putting it mildly. *"Finland?!"* I shouted. "Get him back here now!" The poor man grabbed another phone, and after a short conversation he told me, "They're aborting the takeoff and returning to the gate." Thirty minutes later they brought Charlie and his crate to me. Relieved to be rid of us both, the manager hurried us to the waiting limousine. I never did find out why a crate clearly marked for New York should be put on a plane for Finland. Fortunately, Charlie seemed none the worse for the experience. My nerves recovered and my good humor had returned by the time we arrived at the hotel.

Wherever we went, Charlie lapped up his starring role. Limousines drove us from the airports to our hotels, where there was always a welcoming committee waiting to greet us with special treats for Charlie. Everyone wanted to see and pat this famous dog who had fended off polar bears.

Once at a book signing, a baby nestling in her mother's arms began to cry. Charlie immediately rose from his place at my feet and went to the baby, clearly upset to hear the crying. The baby's mother allowed Charlie to press his nose against her tiny hand. The baby immediately stopped crying and Charlie, satisfied that the baby was all right, returned to sit at my side. His love of people and his gentleness toward them was a source of pleasure not only for Bill and me but for the many people he met in schools and other public events where I was a speaker.

The Arctic tundra in the springtime - wolf country
We can sense the presence of wolves

Chapter Fifteen —
Charlie and the Wolves

Charlie had a unique relationship with wolves too, which we explored in a year-long adventure a few years later. Its seeds were planted back at Resolute on the day after Charlie and I returned from our expedition to the Pole, when I let him free to romp in the ice-covered bay. Soon he spied six juvenile wolves a few hundred yards out on the ice. He gleefully dashed to greet them as if meeting old friends. A game of chase began. "The hamlet's pups grow up knowing wild wolves," Bezal said as he stood with me on the shore watching Charlie. "Wolves come when they catch the scent of seal meat when the dogs are fed. We know that Charlie's grandfather was an Arctic wolf. That's why he plays with them. He knows them." An hour later Charlie returned, tired but happy.

As I watched, I thought of a dream that Bill and I had years before, of observing wild wolves in a truly wild environment. It had seemed only a remote possibility because wolves avoid humans whenever possible. But could our dream become a reality through Charlie's wolf genes? Many studies had been conducted on wolves in a captive-like setting, but we wanted to observe them in a year-long study in their natural environment. A potent symbol of the wilderness, wolves could become an educational program for Adventure Classroom and could take into the classroom the intertwined relationship of the gray wolf species *(Canis lupus)* and other animals that share the wolf's habitat.

Over several years, Bill and I had spent many months exploring remote areas of Alaska, Canada's Yukon Territory, the Northwest Territories, and Nunavut, where we encountered repeated examples of wolves coexisting with other species. When we trekked with the Western Arctic caribou herd to document their spring migration in Alaska, we saw wolves following the half million animals as they streamed north to their calving grounds. In another year, we watched wolves traveling with the Porcupine caribou herd on their four-hundred-mile migration north to their calving area in Alaska's Arctic National Wildlife Refuge. In the northern polar regions, we had seen wolves and Arctic foxes following polar bears far out from land across the sea ice in apparent harmony with each other.

Soon after Charlie and I arrived home, I described to Bill the scene I had watched as Charlie and the wolves had played together. Bill thought that it might work, although we both realized that it would be an experiment and could be fraught with danger for Charlie. We understood that wolves that were strangers to Charlie might not view him as a friend. A wolf pack might drive him away as they would a strange wolf or a dog and might even attempt an attack. To our knowledge no one had ever attempted to use a dog as a go-between. We agreed that above all else Charlie's safety was important, and at the slightest hint of trouble we would abandon our plan.

In 1992 Bill and I skied to the magnetic North Pole, each pulling our own sleds without the aid of a dog team, snowmobile, or aircraft, just as I had four years earlier. We resisted the temptation to take Charlie with us. He had already risked his life protecting me. Now that Bill and I would be a two-person team, we decided that rather than expose Charlie to danger again we would rely on each other. We were well armed with a shot gun and a flare pistol each and a good supply of ammunition. Charlie remained safe at home on the farm with his canine friends. After our successful ski journey to the Pole we returned to base camp, where we happened to meet Ian Randle, a noted British biologist who had come to study Arctic wolves. Over dinner, Ian he said he knew of instances when dogs and wolves had shown respect for each other. While warning us of possible difficulties and dangers to Charlie, and noting that our idea had never been tried before, he thought there was a chance that it might work due to Charlie's inherited wolf genes.

We phoned our *Inuk* friend John Siku, a wolf biologist who lived in Canada's far north and had studied wolves over many years in remote areas all over northern Canada. He was immediately enthusiastic when we described our plans and agreed that it was worth a try, although just as Ian had, John warned, "Wolves might not take to Charlie and could try to kill him. But if you're cautious it might work. You'll have to approach a den very slowly so that the wolves can get a clear look at Charlie. It won't take them long to decide whether to accept him or chase him off."

With John's help we were sure of two good winter wolf locations. John had spent each winter for the last several years studying a wolf pack on the Mackenzie River Delta close to the remote, far northern town of Inuvik in the Northwest Territories of Canada. Then on seal hunts, he had watched a wolf pack following polar bears when the bears hunted on the sea ice of the Beaufort Sea on the southern edge of the Arctic Ocean. Choosing a summer location was more difficult. After some discussion, John told us of a den in the Richardson Mountains in the Canadian Yukon. "It'll be a challenge to find it, but if you can climb through some rough, steep country you'll find a den that's almost unreachable by hunters. I've known this pack for several years. I've camped there and seen them myself. They've seen me so many times they know me."

John was a tall, slender, reserved man who had spent fifteen years living and working in the southern Yukon city of Whitehorse before moving to Cambridge Bay. Once an ardent wolf hunter, he had undergone a life-changing experience when he happened upon a thin, sad-eyed female wolf tied with a heavy ten-foot chain to a fence in a dismal backyard. He bought the animal for fifty dollars, named her Lucky, and turned her loose into the wild. When he released her from the large dog-carrying crate she ran, then stopped and looked back at him with upturned lips as if smiling her thanks. He watched her disappear and vowed never to hunt wolves again. "I'll never forget her expression and the look in her eyes," he told us. "She trusted me. I'll never betray her trust as long as I live." Now his whole life revolves around wolves, their lives, and their protection.

The next summer we set out with Charlie to find the den John had described. If successful, we planned to return the next year to camp as close to the den as the wolves would allow. The Canadian Yukon is wild and mostly uninhabited. Vast expanses of flat and rolling tundra silently sweep the spaces between mountain ranges. Here and there, stunted, twisted stands of black spruce struggle to penetrate the permafrost—a continuous layer of frozen earth ranging from a few feet thick to two thousand feet thick—as the roots seek nutrients from the frozen soil. As summer gradually slips into winter, the tundra turns a dazzling red, orange, and yellow as its foliage prepares for winter. Radiant displays of northern lights, or aurora borealis, grace the dark winter heavens. When snow begins to fall, the tundra's tiny plants, some of which grow only a few inches in a hundred years, become dormant. The land's many moods, its challenges, and most of all its peace have always attracted us.

After days spent traversing wide-open tundra plains, we reached the foothills of the Richardson Mountains. The route described by John took us through rough, steep terrain, where we caught sight of Dall sheep and moose. Charlie traversed all with the skill of a gymnast. At the first sighting of Dall sheep, he instantly charged to the end of his lead with excited barks, whereas the moose warranted only a casual look. We wondered if it was the sheep's white fleece that attracted him, just as it had seemed with Snowy, the white goat back home on the farm.

Following the rough map John had sketched for us, we crested a windswept rocky ridge and looked down into a valley. There, two hundred feet below, we saw a den dug into the base of the far mountainside. Staying carefully concealed, downwind, and silent, we watched wolves come and go on well-worn paths. This area of the valley looked as if they had inhabited it for many generations. Charlie watched with us. He stood looking down with his tail fanning back and forth, excited to see wolves. Already it was clear that his wolf genes gave him an advantage in understanding these animals.

The almost inaccessible valley was perfectly hidden in the surrounding ridges and peaks and concealed from places more easily reached by hunters. A gentle stream meandered through. It was the perfect place, if we could persuade the wolves to accept Charlie and his human companions. After returning home we spent the next few months planning, and then set out in the spring, intent on camping through the summer and fall close to the den. Later, with the arrival of winter, we would travel north to the Canadian Arctic to study the two wolf packs that John had located.

Mother wolf keeps watchful vigil on the newcomers

Chapter Sixteen —
Making Friends

In early April 1994 we set off from the Dempster Highway, a rough gravel backcountry road that ran through the Richardson Mountain foothills. Our eager anticipation was tinged with worry that we might be taking on something that would prove impossible. With a happy Charlie in the lead, Bill and I headed off across the trackless tundra with overly full packs to trek to the wolf den we had discovered a year earlier.

One morning two days into our journey, we were jolted awake by the sound of rustling outside our tent. I froze, listening. Charlie, who had been sleeping in the tent, growled. Moments later, a nearby metallic crash shattered the early morning silence. Charlie's warning grew louder as he snarled, straining at the end of his leash, trying to get through the tent door to face what we guessed was a bear rummaging through our camp. The animal was attacking our cooking gear with gusto. By the sounds of the racket, he was dramatically shortening the useful life of our pots and pans. Bill grabbed the shotgun. Cautiously, he unzipped the main tent door while I opened the back. I looked out and immediately retreated in horror. I was inches from the brown furry side of a large, angry grizzly.

Without seeing me, he bounded around toward the front of the tent. With the barrel barely clearing the doorway, Bill fired a shot into the air. The ear-splitting boom at first had no effect, but after a second deafening warning blast the bear loped a few feet into the nearby taiga forest. Rising on his rear legs to get a better view of us, he paused, then dropped to all fours and lumbered away. Having scrambled out of the tent with us, Charlie continued to growl and strain at the end of his lead, trying to chase after the bear. Long after he had disappeared, Charlie stood guard and never took his eyes from the direction the bear had headed. This was Charlie's first encounter with a grizzly. Apparently in his world a bear of any color was a bear worth chasing, because he had reacted just as he had with polar bears.

Over the next few days we skirted several beaver ponds. With a loud slapping of their tails on the water's surface they warned their families of our unwanted approach. One day a bald eagle looked quizzically down at us from his lofty perch on a branch above us when we cut through a forest of spruce trees to avoid a boggy marsh and a nearby stream teeming with small fish. Charlie stopped to look up, apparently surprised to see a large bird that he had never seen before. But then after a few moments he walked on apparently finding the bird not worth more than a short pause as he led us onward.

A few nights later, about midnight, Charlie suddenly woke us. Standing rigid and alert, he listened to something that sounded like paws crossing the mossy ground at the side of the tent. Bill whispered, "Watch the back door, I'll go to the front." Then we heard a soft yip. Wolves! Now we understood Charlie's absolute quiet. He knew wolves had surrounded the tent, and although he was used to wolves in the Arctic, he had chosen a respectful silence around these strangers. More soft careful footsteps circled us, followed by loud sniffing at the base of the front door, only inches from Bill's crouched, tense body. Probably one of our visitors was trying to discover the contents of our home. Soon the footsteps faded. Charlie slowly relaxed, then lay down, still alert, on my now-empty sleeping bag. Eager to investigate, Bill and I stepped outside. A full moon glowed in a starry sky, lighting the night and casting long shadows across the nearby spruce forest. Deep within the woods, an owl hoot pierced the stillness, followed by an answering nearby hoot. I wondered what these owls were saying to each other.

As we started back to the tent, a long, richly toned howl surged from the shadows, followed by a higher-pitched howl joined by several other voices. We spun to face the trees as the eerie chorus carried through the treetops and faded away, only to start all over again farther away with another long howl. Chills coursed down my spine. At the first howl Charlie had instinctively come to our side. As the howls subsided, he sent a soft *woof* in reply. We strained to see, but could only imagine what was out there. A sudden loud hoot from an owl made my heart race, while Bill visibly jumped. Only Charlie was unperturbed. He wandered off to the tent to once more claim most of my sleeping bag. At first light we discovered the wide paw prints of several wolves in the soft snow. The tracks surrounded our tent and led away to follow a well-worn trail that disappeared into a shaded ravine. After sniffing the tracks Charlie eagerly marked his territory just as we guessed the wolves had marked theirs during the night. We marveled at his copious supply of urine as he went about the careful business of marking his boundaries and making his presence known. Only then did he turn his attention to breakfast. For the next three days we sensed rather than saw wolves keeping an eye on us as we entered their territory and closed in on their den. All the while Charlie seemed relaxed and often looked toward the trees, as if he knew there were wolves close by but felt no need to make a big deal about it.

Our trek continued through deep, sunless valleys, and we spent an entire day climbing over stark, windswept summits two thousand feet high. We traversed precarious caribou trails that clung to the steep mountainsides. On a narrow crest of a particularly steep trail Charlie tensed as he spied two wolves below. After a concentrated stare, he sent out a long howl of varying notes to the distant figures. Just before trotting single file into a thicket of dwarfed trees, a big black animal that appeared to be the leader stopped to look up at us and answered with a long, low-toned howl. Charlie replied, but when he received no response, he resumed his journey without looking back. Charlie's howl surprised us; at home he had learned to bark like our other dogs and we hadn't heard him howl for a long time. But now that he was traveling among wolves, he had returned to sounding like a wolf. We were ecstatic. It appeared that Charlie was communicating to some extent with wolves, and so far, there hadn't been any sign of aggression from them. Although it was still too early to be sure, the early signs gave us hope.

Because a pack's hunting territory ranges over many square miles, we were sure these wolves belonged to our target family. To allow the wolves time to accept our approach to their den, we would now change tactics and begin a slow, nonthreatening advance to gain their trust. Around noon, just as we veered around a lichen-covered rock incline, two wolves startled us. Both stood motionless, watching from a treeless rocky outcrop a hundred feet away. One was the same black wolf we had seen earlier; the other was gray. Charlie stopped. For a few moments he calmly returned their steady gaze, then quietly lay in a submissive pose, head resting on his paws, his head half turned away. Following his lead, we sat behind Charlie and looked to the side to demonstrate our own submissiveness. The two stone-still wolves continued their inquiring gaze while we waited for their next move, hardly daring to even breathe. Minutes later, without a sound, they turned and disappeared in the direction of the den. The next morning, after trekking for an hour, we climbed a ridge located a half-mile from the den and anxiously scanned the area with powerful binoculars.

"I see wolves at the den," I said. We could be sure of it now. It was a relief to see that the wolves were using the same den as last year. After scrambling down into the valley below, we camped. We were hoping that if we approached the den area slowly, it would give the wolves time to communicate with Charlie and become used to his two human companions.

Late the following day a black wolf stepped out from the brush, tail curled high, ears forward and alert. Two younger wolves followed, a gray-black and a blond: apparently last year's pups, now teenagers. These two young ones milled about, suspicious and insecure by contrast to the black male, who continued his proud stare. Soon the big male took a few challenging steps toward us, then stopped in a stare-down, his piercing yellow eyes contrasting with his rich black coat. His authoritative attitude and calm posture confirmed that he was the alpha male that reigned supreme over the entire wolf family. His penetrating gaze dug deep into our souls. Meanwhile, Charlie continued to demonstrate a submissive pose while Bill and I remained crouched below the wolves' eye level in a nonthreatening position. After a last hard look at us humans, the alpha—his gaze softening—turned his attention to the passive Charlie. A minute or so later he and the two teenagers, who tossed frequent nervous glances in our direction, trotted back to the den to join the rest of their family. It was a commanding display of the alpha's superior family position. Charlie rose to his feet, carefully marking his territory by urinating in a line a few yards in front of Bill and me. He appeared to be making known his right to be there.

Although we were encouraged by Charlie's exchange with the wolves, especially the alpha, the all-important question still remained. Was Charlie being accepted, and if so, would the pack accept Bill and me? We were cautiously optimistic.

A day later we moved our camp two hundred feet closer. We were now under constant surveillance by the wolves. They sometimes paced back and forth with nervous but not serious alarm. We kept our gaze averted and moved about camp slowly, never looking directly at them, to prevent any panic. Charlie relaxed in the sun and slept, or sat gazing at the neighbors. But whenever the alpha looked across at us, Charlie immediately demonstrated his submissive pose. He seemed careful to acknowledge the alpha's superior position.

After nine days of cautious, unhurried maneuvering, it was time to test the wolves and determine just how close they would allow us to get to the den. We packed our camp and, with our eyes averted and Charlie urgently tugging on his shorter lead ahead of us, edged slowly closer. Instantly, the wolves clustered together to watch. Tension filled the space between us. The alpha male, tail high, ears forward, lips parted in a partial snarl, stepped in front of his family, ready to defend. The rest waited behind him. Suddenly the two youngsters ran from one adult to the other, as if seeking reassurance. While the adults gave short barks of alarm, the teenagers were even more agitated, puffing their cheeks out as if sending us silent messages with each breath of air. We were too close!

Immediately we stepped back, sat down, and looked away. Charlie lay with his chin resting on the ground, also looking away from the wolves. After about five minutes of a submissive pose, we retreated to a narrow moss- and grass-covered meadow a hundred feet from the den. The pack slowly calmed, but remained wary. The alpha's neck mane stood erect as he barked gruffly at us. Two wolves ran from the den area, circled behind us, and stood stiff-legged, watching and barking. We had reached a critical limit in our approach. Beyond one hundred feet we had breached the wolves' comfort zone. For the next hour we sat with Charlie, silent and not moving. In late afternoon, although still somewhat suspicious and on guard, the entire family gradually relaxed. Even the alpha stopped barking and calmed somewhat, although he still stood regarding us with distrust. The two who had circled behind us rejoined the pack and watched us.

"Do you think we've gone too far?" I whispered to Bill. "Maybe we should leave and camp down the valley for a few days to let them calm down."

"They seem to be settling down," Bill whispered back as he cautiously turned to get a better view of the wolves.

"At least that big black fellow has stopped barking. Let's put up the tent and see what happens. If we go slowly with no sudden moves, it might still work," I said, worried at the turn of events. The wolves' concern and heightened nervousness made it obvious that we had been too close to the den. Uncertain what to do next, we cautiously rose and erected the tent, keeping our movements slow and our eyes averted to prevent any show of aggression on our part. Meanwhile, Charlie walked several feet farther away and lay down, this time with his back to the den.

"We'd better copy Charlie and sit awhile. He seems to know more about this than we do," I said. With occasional sideways glances to check on the wolves, we remained quiet and still with our eyes turned away. With tails still curled high over their backs, they watched us with a caution that gradually faded as evening approached.

To avoid startling the wolves, we didn't light our noisy stove but instead ate a cold dinner of food bars. At dusk the wolves relaxed even more. Some lay down, while others wandered around the den area. The alpha male often looked across at Charlie. We thought he was sizing Charlie up, perhaps deciding whether he was friend or enemy. Later, just as dusk settled over our camp, the alpha appeared to relax and we detected the slight movement of his tail as it barely fanned back and forth, we hoped in friendship. A particularly long-legged male stood high on a ridge above the den, looking away from us across the tundra beyond. Perhaps he had accepted us and was looking for prey? Even the teenagers were less suspicious; one picked up a stick and teased the other into chasing him to steal it.

Now that the day's tension had passed, tranquility spread across our camp. We paused to breathe in the fresh scent of spruce trees and admire the lonely splendor of the mountains and ridges surrounding our tiny meadow. I reached for Bill's hand and whispered, not wanting to break the peaceful spell, "I think we've made it." He squeezed my hand and whispered back, "Yes, thanks to Charlie."

Charlie, outside the tent on his long lead, gobbled his dinner in his usual haste, his appetite unaffected by the excitement. Next, he marked his territory by lifting his leg every few yards. To complete his territorial circle, he sniffed a few of the marks he had made, and then vigorously scratched dirt in a few places around the circle. Then he walked over to the tent, and before we could stop him, urinated on the side closest to the den to leave his scent. In seconds the sharp aroma of urine had begun to infuse our wilderness bedroom. With that, he stepped inside the tent, gave a contented sigh, and settled himself down, apparently well satisfied with his day's work. We knew it was all part of claiming his territory, and we gave our own sighs of relief as it seemed now that we had crossed the first hurdle on our way to acceptance.

Although the family lived in a remote, rugged area deep in the mountains, they had an unobstructed view of the nearby ridges and the game trails. The ridge tops allowed sweeping views across the plain where prey would be visible to sharp wolf eyes. From the summits above and around the den, the pack spent many hours watching for prey across the almost treeless tundra and the distant muskeg, an ancient wetland of peat and low plants. A shallow, meandering stream nearby provided a constant supply of water. Several dugouts had been excavated in the rocky slopes beneath overhangs that offered shelter from the sun and rain. Water, the concealed den area, and the surrounding terrain perfectly suited the secretive nature of wolves in the wild. Several well-worn trails led from the den through the nearby forest and valleys, indicating that this was a popular site that had been used for many generations. We guessed that the den's narrow entrance opened into a wider living space farther back into the slope.

"Wolf Camp One," a name that naturally evolved as the weeks went by, would be our home for the entire summer and fall. The meadow, softened by native grasses and mosses, lay nestled between the den ridge and another ridge three hundred feet high and peppered with a few twisted spruce trees. We pitched our tent in the meadow, where we had a clear view of both the den entrance and the main trail leading into nearby taiga forest. From there we could also clearly monitor the wolves' lookout spot high on the ridge above the den, from which they watched for passing prey.

Charlie's longer camp lead allowed him access to all parts of the meadow and even reached to within twenty-five feet of the den entrance. To guarantee his safety at all times and to prevent him from getting too close to the den, when we were at camp we always kept him tethered to this longer lead. We used a shorter lead when we all traveled together to follow the wolves or hike the surrounding ridges and tundra. Charlie continued to add to his territory with more busy scent marking, and although his lead would have allowed him to mark closer to the den, he seemed to understand just how far he could go in that direction. There seemed to be no hint of any challenge from the wolves, so we assumed that there had been some sort of an agreement between them and Charlie over land claims. While in camp Bill and I always kept to our side of Charlie's marks, especially those in the direction of the den. We wanted to reinforce what we hoped was the wolves' impression that we were Charlie's pack and he was our undisputed alpha leader.

After two days, Charlie no longer presented a submissive pose. He stood tall, his tail curled above his back, displaying his alpha status. He had quickly gained the confidence of the pack. Often one or two of the wolves would stroll over to the nearby rocks, and while relaxing in the shade they would watch Charlie. Their casual postures and gentle facial expressions displayed friendliness. Charlie was at home around them and it was plain that he enjoyed their company. At times he begged to be let off his long lead, but we were afraid to grant his wish. We hoped he wasn't too disappointed. Perhaps we were too cautious, but we couldn't chance anything when it came to Charlie's safety. If he'd succeeded in his foray, we had no intention of allowing him to join the wolves. If trouble developed, we would be unable to defend him.

Although Charlie appeared to have been accepted, it took longer for Bill and me to gain the same trust. Gradually the wolves relaxed in our presence, but they were slow to let down their guard. They had accepted Charlie from the beginning; the howls they had exchanged during the days we spent approaching our final campsite now appeared to have been a conversation of testing and then acceptance. But during our first two weeks at Wolf Camp One, at least one of the wolves watched Bill and me at all times. When either of us moved, sharp eyes always followed. At first, we spent considerable time sitting, moving slowly, and feigning disinterest. In these early stages we never looked directly at the den or the wolves. We dared not climb any of the surrounding ridges that would take us above the level of the den, since that might alarm them. To establish trust, they had to see us as nonthreatening.

Charlie had quickly settled into a routine. His activities alternated between eating, dozing, and wolf watching. Mealtime was an important affair never to be missed. His favorite resting spots included a particularly soft mossy area by the stream, a grassy mound near the tent, and a smooth spot close to his scent-marked boundaries that was excellent for observing the wolves' activities. At night, he retreated to his usual place on my sleeping bag. Now and then he wandered to the stream for a few noisy laps of water or he refreshed his boundaries. These carefully laid markers had been thoroughly inspected by every member of the pack on the first day. Although the borders between the two territories were invisible to Bill and me, clearly Charlie and the wolves understood and observed them. The pack had no problem with Charlie; it was the humans who had to gain their trust.

By mid-May, we had become a familiar fixture rather than an intrusion. The wolves responded by going about their lives in a less watchful fashion. They still kept a cautious eye on us, but did so in an increasingly confident, even somewhat friendly manner. Even the young ones relaxed and continued their playful antics once they became accustomed to seeing us close by. It wasn't long before we became so accepted that wolves passed by us on the trails with hardly a sideways glance, and we could explore the area around the den, surrounding ridges, and tundra without causing alarm to our neighbors. I had two large notebooks that by the end of fall were filled cover to cover. We named each family member to make it easier to record details in my notes. Topping the social scale was the alpha male and his female alpha, who were the parents of two new pups. They became Alpha and Mother. The beta animal, a distinctive blue-gray color, we later discovered to be the new pups' main babysitter and even teacher. The name Beta seemed to fit his respected position as the oldest member of the family.

Two mischievous, energetic teenagers, now a year old, often shared duties babysitting the young pups when the rest of the family left on hunting trips. At first, they were wary of the human strangers and seemed not quite sure about Charlie. But it wasn't long before they relaxed and returned to playing games of chase that were a lot more fun than observing the neighbors. After the first week or two they mostly ignored Bill and me and only occasionally watched Charlie. We called them Klondike and Yukon after two northern rivers.

Most of the hunts were led by a magnificent, powerful animal we called Denali. Later John told us that Alpha and Mother were his parents. John had watched Denali develop through his teen years and now as young adult Denali showed no desire to leave his family to form his own pack. He kept a frequent vigil from the ridge tops looking for any passing prey. When not watching for the next meal that might pass by, he often joined in the games of chase with the teenagers, but generally he was the most serious personality of the family.

The bottom layer of the social scale was reserved for the omega wolf, who we guessed might have been cast out from another pack and been accepted by our wolf family. We named him Omega, and throughout the summer we watched him gradually prove his worth and gain the respect of the pack as he climbed in social status.

Each family member had their place on the family's strict social ladder, which played an important role in their daily life. At meal times Alpha and Mother were the first to eat, followed by Beta and Denali. The teenagers were severely punished with growls and nips if they attempted to push in before their elders. Poor Omega—we felt sorry for him. He was the last to eat and sometimes missed out altogether. Yet, as he gained status, we watched him gradually move up the food line.

Two tiny pups, both males, walking on unsteady legs, followed Mother as she escorted them from the den a few weeks after our arrival. When she finally emerged from the den with her two offspring, the entire family erupted in enthusiastic joy as they greeted the mother and the newest family members. Mother was the last one to finally show any degree of trust in Bill and me and even Charlie. We believed that she delayed bringing the pups out of the den for their first glimpse of the outside world due to her concern over the appearance of new neighbors.

We had been in radio contact with John, the wolf biologist, who promised to join us at our camp. One day in late May we heard the faint sound of someone trekking through the nearby willow thicket. It was John. His greeting was short and to the point. "Hello, are the wolves there?" At the sound of his approach they had silently disappeared. As he pitched his tiny green tent alongside ours, John—as optimistic and enthusiastic as ever—said with a sweeping wave of his hand toward the den, "Don't worry, they're there all right. Just being smart and staying hidden while they figure things out. They know me. We just have to relax and give them space and time. They're used to seeing me coming and going and will soon settle down. Let's sit in your tent." Later we all stepped outside to find that the wolves had indeed returned and sat watching our camp. As soon as John appeared, the entire family relaxed, having apparently recognized him as a friend.

Charlie strolled to his scent-marked boundary, and Alpha approached to within a few yards and fanned his tail back and forth in friendship. John watched, amazed. "I've never seen anything like it. This alpha male looks to Charlie as an equal. Those two have bonded like brothers." The next morning, just before the first subtle light of dawn, we awoke to hear John softly singing a tune in his native language of *Inuktitut*, the traditional oral language of Inuit in the Arctic. Climbing out of the tent, rubbing sleep from our eyes, we saw John sitting on a campstool. In a whisper he said, "I'm calling them. Sit and be still and watch." Reaching to take Charlie's lead, John told him, "Charlie, sit by me. We'll talk to your new friends." Minutes later the wolves appeared, all with heads tilted to one side, listening to the gentle tune that carried across the clear, crisp air. We could see by their relaxed postures that they were used to John's singing. We were fascinated to see the communication between John and his wolf friends. Charlie sat at John's side, relaxed, and stared back at the wolves with his head tilted toward John, appearing to also enjoy his singing. Surrounded by the tune's restful tones, tranquility touched all, including Bill and me.

Wilderness had always been a place of peace for us, but now as we listened, we felt a deeper serenity that before this moment we had never experienced. John was an encyclopedia of wolf knowledge. His Inuit heritage gave him a traditional wisdom about not only the wolves but all wild Arctic species.

Charlie picks up wolf scent on the breeze

He looked into their souls and knew them at a level most humans never can. He never tired of watching Charlie and the various ways he interacted with the wolves. "I see him talking to them with his eyes and body," he said. Charlie's dominant strutting about his marked territory also captivated John. "When I first met him, he was a dog," John said. "Now, out here, he's an alpha wolf." As the days went by, we saw that John was right: Alpha did indeed regard Charlie as an equal. With his intimate knowledge of wild creatures, John instantly understood that Charlie was the key to our success with the wolves. "It'll be hard for them to part when you leave," he said one morning. Bill and I had realized this, and we didn't look forward to leaving.

John laughed when he learned that we had named each of our neighbors. "I never thought of naming them. Makes sense though. At least you named them for places that surround them." After he was certain that all was going well for us at Wolf Camp One, he left. He told us, "I need to check up on a wolf pack on the other side of the mountains. Yesterday aerial hunters shot half the family. It's illegal, but it's hard to stop these people." John was employed by the Canadian government, and part of his job was to investigate illegal activities affecting northern Canada's wildlife.

It soon became apparent that the entire family raised the pups. When Mother left with the others to hunt, Beta and the two teenagers took on the role of pup-sitters. Charlie, clearly fascinated by the two little boys, invited them over with soft sounds of welcome. They would wobble over on their short, unsteady legs into Charlie's territory, and he appeared to enjoy their games of fur pulling and even tolerated the sharp tugs on his tail. At first, we were concerned that the adults would show alarm, but they treated it all as perfectly normal. Just as we began to cook dinner one night, a pup appeared outside the den and was quickly joined by his brother. They inspected a small pebble, rolling it around and pushing it with their blunt noses. Suddenly their attention shifted to a raven's black feather on the ground. A battle ensued over who would keep the feather. After a short tussle, one tried to run off with his prize, while the other chased him on his new short legs. They both collided unexpectedly with an unseen rock and promptly sat down.

The teenagers, who appeared to have pup-sitting duties, nudged both little ones back to the den. For the next week the pups were not allowed to wander more than a few feet. Beta kept an eye on both the pups and the teenagers, but Bill and I suspected he was mostly watching to make sure the teenagers performed their pup-sitting duties adequately. As the days passed, the pups spent more time out of the den and were allowed to investigate some enticing rocks a few yards away. These youngsters were the center of the family's attention. While Mother, Beta, and the teenagers spent the most time with them, the rest of the pack was always attentive. Everyone shared parenting duties.

From the beginning Beta appeared as an older, wise family member. He proved to be the pups' teacher and when we saw that he also supervised the teenagers, we realized that he had been their teacher. As the pups grew, he began to take them on longer and longer walks. The teenagers usually accompanied the trio, always walking in the rear while Beta took the lead. Along the way they would stop and inspect an interesting rock or other object that fascinated the two youngsters, with Beta looking on protectively and with infinite patience.

One sunny afternoon, Bill and I had stretched out on our sleeping pads to enjoy a snooze in the meadow, wolf-style. The whining, annoying mosquitoes, disliking that day's breeze, had left us in peace. The only sound was the faint gurgle of the nearby stream. Charlie lay close to his scent-marked boundary, dreaming the afternoon away. The wolves dozed in favorite places in shady nooks.

Suddenly Charlie broke the quiet with soft yipping. We awoke to see a pup pulling Charlie's fur, begging him to play. Charlie rose to his feet and gently nosed the pup toward Mother, who rested alongside the den. At the sound of Charlie's yips, she and the others were instantly on their feet. Charlie nudged the pup as far as his boundary, where he was met by Alpha. Holding our breath, we half-expected trouble, but Charlie had won the pack's trust, even with their most precious possession. Then, after Alpha had returned the pup to Mother, everyone, including Charlie, went back to sleep. Each day the pups expanded their range as they grew stronger. They cautiously approached the stream and tested it with inquisitive noses, then jumped back in alarm when the water splashed their faces. Mother, always close by, ushered them away whenever they were in danger of falling in. As the pups grew older, the two teenagers engaged them in gentle games of tug-of-war, but always allowed the pups to win. The pups were a great source of entertainment for us. Later as they grew and were allowed to eat fresh meat, they wanted to play on top of the food after they had gorged themselves. The adults, seemingly annoyed by the display of bad manners, with a firm swat quickly removed them from the dinner table.

When Mother joined in a hunt, or just left to get away from the kids, Beta and the teenager babysitters kept the pups close to the den and with endless patience played baby games with them—even to the extent of allowing them to launch pretend attacks, grabbing ears and tails with tiny sharp teeth. Sometimes a pup would attack an adult's tail while his brother grabbed the ears. We marveled that the teenagers and Beta retained any ears at all. The pup-sitters regained peace only when they swatted the offenders as a reminder that even babies must follow the rules. Charlie enjoyed the pups' play. He watched them with his soft gaze and, with enticing yips, occasionally invited them to visit when he sat close to his boundary. While still very young, they would wobble over on their unsteady legs and pull his tail. As they grew, they climbed on his prone body and wrestled with his thick wolf-like fur. Then one day one found his ear. As sharp teeth clamped down, Charlie instantly reached out to pin the offender with a large paw. His sibling slid off Charlie's back, landed within reach of Charlie's other paw, and found himself pinned just like his brother. They were allowed to break free only after considerable squirming. They swung to attack again, but Charlie decided that it was time for the game to end. He stood, looked in the direction of the den, and sounded two yips that brought Mother and Beta on the run. They each picked up a pup and carried him home.

When the pups were tiny, Charlie would roll onto his back with all four paws in the air, allowing the pups to climb over him and grab mouthfuls of fur. With fierce puppy growls they pulled and wrestled with the fur until Charlie decided that enough was enough and abruptly stood, sending his two miniature tormentors tumbling. One day they followed Charlie to the stream and bent to copy him as he drank. One almost fell in and accidentally dunked his head under water. Instantly regaining his balance, he made puppy squeals that could be heard by the sleeping adults. Charlie led both back to his boundary right away, and they scampered across to join their mother, who was basking in the warm afternoon sun. She briefly raised her head, but seemed unconcerned. It looked as if she trusted Charlie to get them back home safely. We were delighted that the family's trust in Charlie even extended to the pups. But as they grew and lost their baby habits and their games became more boisterous, he no longer invited them to play and was content to watch their antics from a distance. When they approached his boundary, he informed them with soft but authoritative growls that he preferred that they observe his property rights. They were quick to learn their limits and turned back to find another nearby victim.

Of course we didn't know the rules, but we could tell that a set of rules existed about the pups. Concerned that if they spent too much time with Charlie it might impair our relationship with the family, we often shooed them back home. At first, when very young, unsteady on short legs, and with uncertain eyesight, they would wander over Charlie's boundary and head in Bill's and my direction. We knew it was important that we never touch them and leave our scent on their bodies, so with much shouting and shooing, we sent them home. As their eyesight improved and they could better recognize their surroundings, they soon learned that we were not new playmates.

Bones in various stages of chewed destruction lay around the wolves' living area. After returning with Beta from forays to nearby ridges, the fast-growing pups would spend a substantial amount of time chewing some of these leftovers, while others became toys. One day a pup, with Charlie looking on, carefully dug a shallow hole behind one of Charlie's scent-marked rocks and buried a large moose leg bone. After the pup joined his brother and Yukon for a game of chase, Charlie dug up the bone and carried it to the side of the tent, where he promptly lay down and chewed it. Ownership had changed.

The habit of burying is part of life with a dog and Charlie was no exception. One night full of the sound of rain and wind, we cooked dinner and slid into our sleeping bags, intent on staying warm while we caught up on our journal notes. But first we had to look for Bill's reading glasses. Such things as gloves, socks, and eyeglasses disappear into the jumbled void of a tent's contents with exasperating frequency, we have found. Even though Bill testily claimed that they had to be in a side pocket, just where he put them, the pocket was empty. After going through just about everything, I triumphantly found the glasses—squashed but still usable—beneath Charlie, who had watched us placidly during the search, but never moved a muscle. Only as a last desperate measure had I slid my hand beneath his heavy body. "Charlie, you knew they were there all the time!" Bill exclaimed as he made an adjustment to the slightly bent frame.

My journal writing prompted some interesting interactions with the wolves. One day a loose page from my journal fluttered on the breeze to land two feet over Charlie's scent-marked boundary line. Normally Bill and I were very careful not to cross the line except when leaving our campsite, when we crossed it at the most distant point from the den. The page contained my notes carefully describing a howling session. Without thinking, I crossed the invisible boundary and bent to pick up the page, but looked up just as my hand reached the paper. Alpha had silently approached and stood three feet away. He glanced at the page for a moment and then, with his head cocked to one side, his yellow eyes met mine with a softer but inquiring expression. I straightened slowly and stepped back. Alpha stepped forward, took the page in his mouth, and turned to walk away. I hoped I could get him to drop the notes. They represented many hours of work, and I wasn't about to give them up without protest. I extended my hand, "Alpha, that page is mine," I said softly. At the sound of my voice, he stopped and looked back. His steady eyes held mine for a moment. Keeping my hand extended, I continued to speak to him in quiet, even tones. With his gaze still fixed on mine, he dropped the paper and then strolled to a shady rock with a barely perceptible fanning of his tail. Alpha could easily have kept my precious notes as a display of dominance, but he chose to treat me as a friend instead. I picked up the notes and walked back to the tent. I needed to absorb what had just happened. It was a moment so special and unexpected that it would be stamped on my mind forever.

One day in midsummer, the pack spent most of the day hunting and returned just as evening's dark shadows crept across the valley. They were gathered around Beta and seemed to be urging him on. Then we saw that he hobbled on a badly injured paw, which we assumed had been injured in a moose hunt. He lay at the den entrance while others sat at his side and licked the wound. Over the next few days he was never left alone until able to walk with barely a limp. Meanwhile, as he recovered, hunters brought food and laid it at his side. Watching the care given by the entire family—their unfailing devotion not only to their injured companion but also to each other, combined with the pack's strong family ties and intense loyalty—made us consider our own human attitudes. In the quiet of the mountains and valleys surrounding us, it was easy to think and care like a wolf and to at least begin to see life as they saw it. Not only were we learning of the ways of wild wolves and how they lived in a place as harsh and remote as the Yukon, but we were learning about ourselves.

Wolves enjoy a splash in the creek

Charlie - The Hero by My Side

Those pesky ravens

Credit: Marlin Greene

Chapter Seventeen —
The Ravens

A noisy flock of ravens had taken up residence in the spruce trees and crevices in the cliffs close to the wolf den. We were impressed with the intelligence and cunning of these birds. Wolves and ravens are both sociable creatures, and although we would have thought them to be unlikely companions, they appeared to enjoy each other's company. The ravens liked to tease the wolves and sometimes initiated play with individuals. While the wolves dozed comfortably one day, a raven appeared as silently as a shadow, landing a few feet from Klondike. It sneaked up behind her, pausing now and then to make sure it had not been detected. When the raven reached the end of Klondike's tail, the bird gave a quick jab with its large beak, then quickly flew away with a loud squawk and perched atop a six-foot-high rock.

Klondike leaped to her feet in indignation. Seeking revenge, she made futile attempts to scramble up the steep rock. But she slid to the ground each time, her claws leaving long scratches in the soft rock. Then the raven flew onto the ridge and watched for further opportunities. After a few minutes a disgruntled Klondike gave up and resumed her sleep but now in the protection of a nearby dugout.

Not even Charlie was spared. One day as he lay alongside the stream, two ravens crept up behind him in waddling unison and, as if on cue, both nipped his tail at once. With a loud yelp Charlie jumped up, ready to kill, but the clever birds flew to the ridge, where they strutted and cawed, elated at their success. Charlie's indignant bark brought all the wolves to watch and, we supposed, to sympathize as he railed against his tormentors. Another time, when Charlie was engrossed in eating his dinner, three ravens acting as a team swooped down from the cliff. A particularly bold individual led the attack, diving at Charlie's head. When he left the bowl to race after the first bird, the others made for the abandoned food, stealing as much as they could grab in their large beaks in one low pass. The infuriated Charlie angrily turned and leaped at the ravens. But even though he reached a height he had perhaps never before attained, he was too late. We allowed him to eat inside the tent from then on.

One evening as the sun sat low in the sky, Charlie was reclining comfortably at his favorite spot beside the stream. Bill and I were relaxing, taking in the tranquility of a perfect evening. Suddenly Bill nudged me and pointed to Charlie. Mesmerized, we watched, fascinated by the event unfolding before us. Three ravens were cautiously sneaking up behind Charlie with malicious intent, while he was watching with half-closed eyes, feigning sleep. Suddenly there was a violent eruption of black fur mixed with black feathers. From a reclining start Charlie had leaped straight up in the air and come down on top of a panicked raven. He tried with all his might to grab the unfortunate bird, which fought to escape from beneath his furry body. His loud growls and the bird's panicked squawks completely destroyed the tranquility of the evening. After what seemed an eternity, the unfortunate creature, writhing and fighting in desperation, finally broke free and, with one powerful flap of its wings and a squawk that radiated sheer panic, sought sanctuary on the nearby ridge. A few black feathers floated down to earth as Charlie raced to the base of the ridge. He finally gave up and returned to the tent where, with a disgruntled look, he disappeared inside for the night. As for the raven, it was apparently so traumatized that it could only sit silently as it preened and rearranged its disheveled feathers. Meanwhile, its two companions had flown to the ridge in terror as soon as they saw their companion's plight. Even they were silent, as if they regretted the whole episode.

From then on, we noticed that the birds were careful to keep a safe distance from Charlie, now that he had displayed impressive athletic ability and had come close to victory. Instead, they developed a new tactic of ganging up and strutting back and forth well out of reach. As if teasing him in revenge, they kept up a continuous loud annoying chatter until he made a fruitless charge in their direction. Of course, they had it all well planned and quickly flew just out of reach to land on a convenient ledge, where they continued their noisy commotion. Eventually an agitated Charlie, his loathing for these infuriating birds all too obvious, would give up in disgust and retreat to his refuge inside the tent.

Even Bill and I sometimes grew tired of the noisy birds and shooed them away. Of course, Charlie treated these occasions as his personal victory and gleefully joined in our quest to convince the birds to take their irritating racket elsewhere. The ravens showed little fear of Bill and me, becoming unbearably bold at times as they strutted and waddled about our campsite with impunity. With heads tipped sideways, they peered at us with their beady black eyes and talked nonstop—about us, we were sure. A few times the birds dived low over our heads, knocking off our caps. They even landed on the tent and pecked the fabric as if to tease us. As a precaution, we kept all our food inside, away from both wolves and birds. It wasn't long before we dared not leave small items outside the tent. Nothing was safe from these impudent birds, which displayed a talent for stealing when our backs were turned. As time went on, we saw that the ravens and the wolves appeared to be socially connected. Twice we watched ravens rouse the wolves by flying low and emitting loud squawks. As soon as the birds had gained the wolves' attention, they flew back and forth until the wolves followed them to the source of their excitement, which we guessed must be carrion in the forest or on the tundra.

Once during the endless daylight of summer, we left camp with Charlie at two in the morning, hoping to watch the wolves hunt. We had positioned ourselves on a low rise about three hundred yards away with an unobstructed view of the wolves' living area. We were hoping that if we started closer to the prey, our head start would enable us to follow the wolves for at least part of the distance to their hunting site. With some luck we might even see the actual hunt. At the den ravens circled overhead squawking loudly, trying to gain the wolves' attention. Denali, who had been scouting from the lookout on his favorite ridge since midnight, raced down the slope to greet Alpha with vigorous tail wagging. Beta and Omega quickly joined them. After a few minutes of excited milling about, these four wolves, led by Denali, trotted along the main path from the den and disappeared into the trees with the ravens flying overhead, appearing to lead the hunters to the tundra beyond the trees. They headed north with the ravens circling overhead. Now and then the ravens waited in the treetops for the hunting wolves to catch up. They appeared to be leading the wolves to some sort of prey.

We jogged along an easy shortcut across the tundra, then traversed a steep slope. Cresting a low ridge, we saw below us a moose already dead, perhaps from old age or sickness. A few ravens, already perched on the carcass, cawed loudly. In the next minute more ravens were circling overhead. Almost immediately the wolves burst from low undergrowth and straightaway began the task of ripping open the moose hide. The ravens now joined in the feast. It was clear to us that the ravens had led the wolves to the carrion and waited for them to break open the carcass, which had proved impossible for them even with their large sharp beaks. Because of the birds' inability to tear open a tough-skinned carcass, they needed the wolves to do the job for them. We marveled at this remarkable display of interdependence and food sharing by two very different wild species. The folklore of the First Nations people of northern Canada contains many legends that extol the supernatural life of this bird. Raven is a powerful figure, responsible for making rivers flow, bringing daylight to the world, hanging the moon in the sky, and acquiring fire. Legend says that he created people, and then tricked them out of their food.

Mystical powers have been attributed to ravens as far back as ancient Greece. Odin, the raven god and ruler of the Norse gods, kept a wolf on each side of his throne and a raven on each shoulder. Wolves and ravens even accompanied Odin into battle.

"Remember Billy McCaw and what he told us about the ravens?" I said as we watched. Billy was a wise elder of the *Gwich'in* First Nation whom we had met two years before. He had told us that wolves and ravens talked to each other. So old he could not remember his own age, Billy had spoken to us in a raspy voice with a faraway look in his faded eyes. "Ravens call the wolves and lead them to prey," he said. "They depend on the wolves to break open the carcass. Ravens will call the wolves to an injured animal too. After the wolves eat, the birds take what's left. They know more than all the animals in the north." When I asked him if wolves helped humans to hunt, he had replied, "Sometimes they do. It is said that they will help only those who respect them. It is said that a long time ago my grandfather's dogsled overturned and he hurt his leg. Ravens who'd followed him on the hunt flew two miles back, and screeched and circled until his brother paid attention and followed them to my grandfather. Many of our elders can tell you when a raven is serious and is talking. Ravens are our friends. We should listen to them." Now we understood what Billy had meant. From then on these intelligent birds, which until now we had regarded only as bothersome nuisances, had our lasting respect.

Photos around the den

Helen and Bill say goodbye — time to leave

Chapter Eighteen —
Goodbye

Eventually fall settled over the mountains. The season we dreaded had arrived. It was time to leave Wolf Camp One and travel to Inuvik, where John would meet us, and start our winter project. We wondered how Charlie would react to leaving his friends.

A bitterly cold wind swept through the mountains from the north as we prepared to leave. Temperatures dropped into the 20s and a skim of ice covered the ponds, while shallow pools were frozen solid. Snow covered the mountains in a white mantle. Yellow leaves drifted to earth, and fiery red tundra plants disappeared beneath the snow. The shimmering greens, pinks, and blues of the aurora borealis, or northern lights, were visible in the lengthening darkness. The Arctic winter's deep cold had begun its slow march across the land.

The well-fed wolf pack was in a healthy condition, ready for the winter. With increasing frequency, the pups traveled longer distances from the den under strict supervision, sometimes for most of the night and all day. Packs normally leave the den area at the beginning of winter, so we knew the entire family would soon be departing to hunt and travel the full range of their territory. The two pups, now resembling teenagers, would go with them. With their pups accompanying them, wolves can travel over a much wider area in winter, since they don't have to return to den sites until spring. Then at winter's end the group either returns to an old site, as this family had, or digs a new den in another area to accommodate the next litter of pups.

We couldn't remain emotionally distant from these intelligent, wild hunters who at times acted like playful children. We had grown attached to these animals, who showed us the importance of deep family ties and devotion to each other. And we appreciated how much they had taught us. They had captured our hearts. Leaving was sad for all of us, but it was particularly difficult for Charlie. Although utterly bonded to Bill and me, he had become very wolf-like and enjoyed being with the wolves. When we began dismantling our camp, Charlie sensed that we were leaving. He walked over to his boundary close to the den and gave a mournful howl that radiated sadness. The entire pack, even the pups, came closer. They all sensed that we were preparing to leave. Bill and I spoke to the wolves. We knew we made no sense to them, of course, but we hoped we might communicate our love and respect. One by one I called them by their names and said goodbye. Bill did the same. "We won't forget you," he said, his voice subdued with sadness.

Lifting the heavy packs and sliding into the shoulder straps, we sadly turned to go. I tugged Charlie's lead, but he refused to budge. He stood facing the wolves. Then we sat with him and cried. The only way we could leave them was to know that we would see them again. Weeks before, we had decided to return with John for a brief visit the next summer and for several more to make sure they remained safe from hunters. Fighting tears as we looked across at the watching group, I said to Bill, "If only we could know they will come to no harm, it would be easier." We had already talked about how we could protect the family and concluded that we would do as John did: keep the den's exact location a secret forever. While Bill held Charlie close, I explained, "Charlie, winter's here. We have to leave. We can't leave you behind." He seemed to sense our emotions. Reluctantly he turned to leave, then stopped and looked back at his friends for a few minutes.

Then, with a quick little touch to my hand, he followed at my side. With the wolves watching, we left the wild family we had almost become a part of and the meadow we had called home for six months. We stepped across the stream and saw Mother and the pups sitting dejectedly on our tent's spot. The two teenagers, who had grown into elegant adults, joined the pups. In unison they all raised their voices to the sky and sent out a long, sorrowful howl that echoed off the mountainsides. Alpha yipped twice. Then, accompanied by Beta, Denali, and Yukon, they followed us for the next three hours. As we crossed a ridge, Charlie stopped and raised his muzzle for one last howl with his friends. They all howled together for ten minutes, a sound that broke our hearts.

Then the wolves turned away to return to their den. Charlie watched until they had disappeared. Finally, they were gone. A dejected Charlie led us away, his tail and head held low in sadness. Bill and I followed in silence. Although we knew we would return for a visit next summer, it was one of the saddest days of our lives, and we could see that Charlie shared our sorrow. For the next three days Charlie, his manner quiet and despondent, consented to nibble a few treats but refused to eat his meals. By the fourth day he seemed to have accepted our parting from his friends and returned to his normal buoyant self. But leaving his friends behind had been a difficult hurdle for him. It was only his close bond to Bill and me that had persuaded him to leave.

Full winter gear on the Arctic ice again

Winter camp on the Arctic ice

Chapter Nineteen —
Ice Wolves

Now to travel to the far north and meet John. After gathering supplies in Inuvik, and with John's directions and written notes in hand, we left the northern Canadian coastline behind us. We skied, pulling our sleds onto the windswept ice of the Beaufort Sea, and headed north to locate the coordinates that John had given us, where we hoped to see the wolves and polar bears that John had been studying over the previous several winters.

During several Arctic expeditions, Bill and I had also observed wolves traveling far from land across the sea ice, seemingly in contact with polar bears. The question we wanted to explore was why wolves would travel where their normal land prey does not exist. Why do they go onto the sea ice far from shore?

At first, we were confronted with a precarious jumble of massive slabs and blocks of ice strewn about by ocean currents that rose and fell under the great weight of the ice. Charlie was happy to be back on the sea ice and raised his nose whenever he detected the enticing scent of seals. Each time we crossed polar bear tracks, he pulled hard on his lead as he anticipated the possibility of once more engaging in his favorite sport, pursuing bears. When we insisted that we all continue northward, his look of abject misery sent us the message that we sorely lacked even the most basic understanding of his need to indulge in a good bear chase.

Our destination was an area John had identified as a region of thinner ice that often resulted in numerous water-leads—places where the ice had split apart, exposing the ocean's water where seals made their home in the frigid watery depths.

On the second day we reached an uneven area of ridges, twenty feet high, split by narrow gaps that were barely wide enough to pull our sleds through. At times we had no option but to haul our heavily laden sleds up and over the top of the ridges and drop them down the other side, always careful not to step on a particularly unstable block of ice that could send us tumbling back down to where we had started. Charlie had no such problem. As nimble as a champion gymnast, he leaped from block to block and always reached the top long before we did. Just as I pulled my sled through an exceptionally tight gap that almost jammed it, the ice suddenly groaned as it settled and moved with the ocean currents. Blocks the size of small cars toppled as if they were toys. The ice was on the move. Bill yelled, "Leave the sleds and get out!" Dropping my sled harness, I scrambled down just as another great groan rumbled through the ice, toppling even more blocks. Charlie leaped the gaps to follow close at our heels. From the relative safety of a flat ice pan, we watched the sleds sway among the unstable blocks that threatened to crush them. After fifteen minutes, there was silence. Was it safe and still now? We scrambled back to our sleds, praying that the ice wouldn't shift and crack open. We grabbed the sled ropes, jerked the sleds free, and hauled them to flat stable ice. Convinced that things had settled down, we headed north but had taken only a few steps when we heard a deep rumbling. Quick as lightning, a split opened ten feet behind us. With a rush of adrenaline, we dashed in the opposite direction, toward what looked like stable ice. Huge cracks cut through the surface at our heels as we ran. One suddenly appeared three feet ahead. We hurdled it, still dragging our sleds. As the sound grew to thunderous proportions, an anxious Charlie ran with us, leaping the cracks. Terrified, we all ran at least a half mile before the vibration and deafening noise subsided enough to allow us to stop, completely out of breath but glad to have escaped the jaws of the breaking ice. Clearly concerned at the turmoil that had erupted around us, Charlie stayed at my side as if to gain some measure of reassurance.

There was enough daylight left to escape the area before nightfall. We turned east in search of a safe route and encountered day-old bear tracks mixed with the smaller prints of foxes. Charlie sniffed the tracks, caught the bear scent, and tugged at his lead. He had already forgotten our race to safety and was now intent on pursuing his favorite pastime, polar bear chasing. "Forget it, Charlie," I said. "We have more important things to do." A sharp pull on his lead persuaded him to follow, but not without a short bark of protest. Two hours later and six miles out of our way, we reached the end of the ridges and could see several miles of level ice ahead. We stopped for a quick snack, but with the temperature hovering at minus 41 degrees we resisted the temptation to take a longer break.

Later, cold and tired, we stopped to make camp. Only Charlie seemed to have energy to spare as he set about investigating fox tracks. Intent on fox hunting, he was delighted when we released him from his lead. With nose to the ice, he dashed away to follow a particularly enticing track that led to low slabs of ice close by. Two foxes, suddenly aware of a pursuer, raced away in panic as Charlie threw himself into the chase with a frenzy of a dedicated hunter. But he was no match for the lightning speed of the foxes. After a futile search for his victims, which by now had vanished, he abandoned his chase. When he saw that the tent was erected and we were unloading gear, he immediately changed course and headed into the tent to look for my sleeping bag, which he considered his personal property.

For the next two days—and with a happy Charlie in the lead—we regularly crossed bear, wolf, and fox tracks, all traveling from one seal breathing hole in the ice to another. The abundant seal population ensured good hunting for the bears. All of the tracks appeared to be traveling in the general direction of the area that John had described to us as a place of frequent open water leads and a bountiful seal population. The breathing holes of ringed seals were places of sheer delight for Charlie, with delightful seal aromas and occasionally even a few scraps of meat left over from seal kills that he eagerly chewed with gusto.

Charlie yipping to friendly ice wolves

Now that we were traveling across ice heavily populated by polar bears, we kept a 360-degree lookout. Our loaded shotguns lay on top of our sleds, and our loaded flare guns were tucked into our pockets. Charlie always walked at our side, alert to signs of bears, just as he had on my journey with him to the magnetic North Pole.

A few days later, when we'd set up camp and just as Charlie was about to turn his attention to his food bowl, he suddenly whipped around to face the rear and leaped, snarling, to the end of his lead. Sure enough, a bear approached from around three hundred feet away and strode straight toward us. As Charlie's snarls reached a furious crescendo, we grabbed our loaded flare guns and rapidly fired flares to land on the ice in front of the advancing bear. At first, seemingly unimpressed by the flares that were landing almost at his feet, he marched onward. But then as the curtain of flare smoke thickened, the bear raised his nose to test the unfamiliar smell and slowly backed away. He strode in a wide circle around us, defiantly tossing a look back over his shoulder as if unwilling to leave. But eventually Charlie's determined leaping and snarling persuaded him to leave permanently.

The next day, after a blissfully bear-free night, we traveled over a minor ridge and skied across smooth ice. We reached an area of older multi-year ice pinnacles molded and sculptured by nature into shapes delicately curved and tinted green. Some as high as fifteen feet stood blocking the way ahead. Later the surface smoothed to a uniform whiteness, snow and clouds merging into one at the horizon.

At midday we arrived at an area of open water several hundred yards wide. Six seal-hunting bears were pacing the edges, followed by five wolves and numerous foxes who dodged in and out, careful to keep out of range of their larger companions. Two male bears growled nose to nose, testing each other over hunting space. We camped about two hundred yards away, our tent barely screened by a couple of low ice mounds. We reasoned that the animals were too busy searching for seals in the open water to notice us, at least for now. A few years earlier, during a training expedition close to Resolute, we had encountered thirteen bears striding along the edges of sea ice hunting for seals in the nearby open water. We had nervously skirted the area. We weren't prepared to see that many bears in one place. Now, more experienced, we felt cautiously comfortable being so close to these bears. Still, we kept a sharp eye out and our shotguns and flare guns close at hand.

Referring to the notes John had written for us regarding the identifying marks on these wolves, we judged this pack to be the same one John had been studying. Several feet from the water's edge, a large male bear hovered silent and still over a patch of ice. Suddenly he rose on his hind legs and crashed down with enormous front paws to land his full weight over a seal lair. The ice broke. He thrust his head through the opening, yanked out a struggling seal, and dropped it on the ice. In seconds he had crushed the seal's head and torn off thick strips of blubber. A sixth wolf, with a gray-tinted blond coat and a large dark patch on one rump, now stood a few feet away. Occasionally the bear growled a warning to the wolf not to approach his meal. After he had consumed the blubber, the fatty part of the seal, the bear left the meaty carcass and returned to the water's edge. The wolf immediately claimed the body while foxes scampered just out of reach, waiting for leftovers. Thirty minutes later, after the wolf had gorged himself, he left the skeleton and meat scraps for the half-dozen foxes.

We now understood how wolves survived on the sea ice far from land. Our observations agreed with John's—polar bears are the key that enables wolves to live on the sea ice far from land where their normal land-bound prey exists. We theorized that after the sea ice was strong enough to provide a hunting platform for the bears, this wolf pack left the land for the sea ice and followed the bears as they hunted. It appeared that these wolves and foxes had discovered that it is easier to allow the bears to do all the work and wait close by ready to share in the bounty, rather than hunt during the harsh winter months on land, often in deep snow.

While we watched, fascinated by all the activity, Charlie stood a few feet in front of us, his gaze riveted on the bears and wolves. He gave no sign that he was concerned about any possible aggressive behavior by our neighbors. Rather, he appeared to be just as fascinated as we were. Standing outside our tent dressed in our warmest polar jackets, we watched the hunting activities until dark.

Although the blond wolf, whom we called Patch because of his rump mark, seemed to prefer working alone, he joined the other five occasionally. Once, as he approached his companions, they all ran in tight circles. It seemed to be a game in which everyone chased everyone else. Minutes later they all stopped, joined in an enthusiastic display of muzzle licking, then all rejoined the bears as if to see what was being offered for dinner.

We assumed that the wolves had communicated with Charlie in some invisible way that satisfied them that he was a friend and not a foe. We weren't surprised that the wolves had not shown undue alarm at Bill's and my presence. John was confident that due to his own frequent interaction with this pack they would accept us as long as we stayed a comfortable distance away and made no sudden moves. Even when a wolf glanced in our direction, it was apparent—judging by their calm attitude—that they were used to seeing humans. We watched the neighbors until a minus 31-degree cloak of darkness and cold spread beneath the star-lit sky.

We ate cold food so that our noisy stove didn't attract unwanted attention or mask the sound of an approaching bear. Even when we laid Charlie's pan of food before him he ignored it, and instead kept a close watch on the still-hunting bears. Eventually hunger took over, but after he ate his dinner, he stood at the doorway watching, his canine eyes seeing through the darkness.

Not long after nightfall engulfed our campsite, the bears and wolves left to investigate an area of open water a half mile away. Barely able to see them in the moonlight's reflection off the ice, we decided that because we had not so far become the center of either the wolves' or bears' attention, we could safely get some sleep. Charlie, as usual, would warn us of any potential danger. However, we had no sooner settled into our sleeping bags when the sound of quiet sniffing by many noses and the padding of soft footsteps surrounded our tent. An instantly alert Charlie sat tense, listening. Moments later he *woofed* softly, as if in some sort of greeting. Instantly the sniffing stopped. After a pause a single *woof* came in reply. Then, to our surprise, Charlie lay back down and resumed his trip to doggy dreamland, while outside there was only silence. Apparently, our neighbors had come to inspect our abode and then, after a brief communication with Charlie, had left. Now we were certain that these wolves had accepted Charlie.

We stepped out of the tent and saw that the bears had returned to the hunting area closer to our tent site. With bears only a few hundred yards away, it was impossible to sleep even with Charlie on guard. After some discussion we decided to sleep in two-hour shifts, with Bill taking the first shift. Charlie stood with Bill, apparently having also decided that the bears were too close to let his guard down. During my turn I pulled my bulky down parka around me and tucked my hands deeper into my polar gloves. I was surprised that as my eyes grew accustomed to staring into the darkness, I could see the animals moving about in the moonlight.

Now and then the ice spoke its own special language: cracking sounds, long humanlike sighs, and a peculiar whine that built to a frenzied pitch before sliding back down the scale to silence. *The immense frozen ocean was protesting its imprisonment,* I imagined, as the ice moved with the ocean currents. Even with a watchful Charlie at my side I felt very alone. In the gray darkness, my world had shrunk. Pinnacles of ice, impossibly tall in the deceptive light, loomed against the starry sky. I looked to my left, straining to penetrate the dim surroundings. Was it my imagination, or did I really detect a slight movement in the distance? Charlie showed no reaction and continued to keep an eye on the animals still moving around close to the open water. It was a comfort to have him at my side, just as it had been when we had traveled to the Pole.

Later, as though Charlie had decided that all was safe for now, he stepped back into the tent and spread out across my sleeping bag while I continued to stare into the distance, still not sure if something was moving out there. Just I had convinced myself that it was only my imagination, Charlie appeared at my side with hackles raised, his body tense and on guard. He too stared into the distance, apparently sensing a bear. I braced myself and reached for the shotgun and flare gun, but still I saw nothing. After thirty minutes of tense staring into space, Charlie gave a low, sharp woof and disappeared back into the tent. I marveled at and envied his instinctive ability to sense bears, and was thankful for his ceaseless desire to keep Bill and me safe. Bill told me later that on his watch, he caught sight of a far-off bear and a wolf traveling together to the water's edge that night. Charlie stepped out of the tent. But this time, after a short, concentrated stare at the ghostly forms, he relaxed and returned to bed without a sound. Apparently, Charlie understood when the bears' intentions toward us were peaceful, and for the moment sleep was more important than bear watching.

Morning's soft light crept slowly across the ice, and with it came the blessed relief of good visibility. A mother polar bear and two cubs had arrived during the night. To protect her offspring from the males who continued to hunt close by, she stayed a hundred yards away and shared a seal carcass with her cubs. We weren't surprised that day and night were the same to these sea ice hunters, but our eyes were not the same: the good visibility of daylight gave us significantly more confidence.

We stayed another day to watch activities. After Charlie had eaten his breakfast he sat watching as several bears patrolled the ice edge while the wolf family watched in anticipation of a meal. Now and then a bear dived into the water and swam after a retreating seal that quickly dived out of reach. Some bears left while others continued to arrive throughout the day. John had told us this was a prime seal hunting area, and he proved to be right, judging by the number of bears and the number of frantically wriggling seals that were hauled from the water. With each successful catch the victors ate their fill while the waiting wolves and foxes gathered close, watching for the first opportunity to grab anything left on the ice.

Later, a large blond male wolf approached the water. A smaller, limping female of slightly darker color followed him. She appeared to have injured a front paw. Meanwhile, a massive bear with three wolves waiting at a respectful distance stood motionless over a seal breathing hole in the ice. Just as the blond male and his companion arrived, the bear thrust his massive head into the hole and hauled out a struggling seal, crushed its head and, without stopping to eat, returned to the edge of the ice and stared into the water. The three wolves accompanying him wasted no time rushing to the body. Several foxes dashed in and out, barely keeping out of reach of snapping wolf jaws. While two wolves gorged themselves, the third one tore off a large chunk of meat and delivered it to the blond male who stood with his female companion fifty feet way. After dropping the meat, he turned back to re-join his feasting companions. Meanwhile the limping female had limped closer. Without taking a single bite, her blond companion took the meat to her. She hungrily grabbed it and gulped it down. Her companion turned back to the three wolves, and as he approached them, the same wolf who had already provided him with the gift of meat once more ripped a large portion off the dwindling carcass and dropped it at the blond wolf's feet. Blondy, as we now called him, chomped down the lot, while the other three finished off the carcass. Fascinated, we continued to watch. After the entire seal carcass had been consumed, the three wolves again shadowed the bear as he stalked the water's edge a quarter mile to the north. Blondy stayed with the female, as if to help her, and both remained within easy distance of their companions, as if to await further gifts of food. We were captivated by the process of food sharing between two animal species. John had watched this process over the last several years and now we had seen it for ourselves.

Polar bears, the primary hunters, killed the prey and then ate mostly the fat. Sometimes the bear ate none of it, and left the entire seal carcass for the wolves. During several years of Arctic expeditions this was the first time we had actually seen this sequence of events, although for some time we had suspected it existed. Charlie, too, appeared captivated by all the activity. Now and then we noticed a wolf turn to look at us and once we saw Charlie's tail give a gentle wave as if in recognition to some sort of canine signal. As with the summer wolves, an understanding of respect had taken place between Charlie and this wolf family.

We had pushed our safety margin to the absolute limit. Next morning, after another tense night, we looked out at first light and saw that the bears and wolves had moved farther to the east to another hunting site. With no animals in sight, we packed up in the last gray light of dawn and skied north in the direction of Richards and Pullen Islands, both named for early Arctic explorers.

After several hours of easy skiing across good ice we approached a twenty-foot-high pyramid of sparkling blue ice. Charlie stopped and yipped several times. Puzzled because the sound was different from his usual bear-warning growls, we allowed him to lead us around to the far side. We froze, incredulous at the sight before us. About two hundred feet away stood a group of eleven wolves, all of whom we had seen on and off since arriving at the open water hunting area. The family alpha male had already detected our approach. He stood stiff-legged, hostile and defensive in front of his family, ready to defend them. The others watched and paced nervously, never taking their eyes off us. We had accidentally placed ourselves too close. Charlie dropped to his belly with his muzzle averted, showing submission, while Bill and I hastily sat on our sleds and looked away hoping to demonstrate that we meant no threat. With a series of barks of various tones, interspersed with growls, the alpha quickly led his entire family away to cluster behind two-foot-high chunks of ice, then stopped to watch us with deep suspicion.

We slowly rose from our sleds, and with Charlie at our side, we retreated to an area of open ice where we were clearly visible. Once again, we sat on our sleds while Charlie lay on his belly, his head turned away in submission. We had surprised the group in a place they frequented regularly, judging by the many patches of urine-discolored snow and numerous wolf scats nearby. After a long tense standoff, the wolves—although still cautious—appeared to relax. The leader barked a short warning but gave no sign of his earlier concern. Charlie, still belly-down on the ice, raised his head and replied with a few yips so soft even we understood they were benevolent. It appeared that the pack had recovered from our unexpected arrival and now the leader stared hard at Charlie. But after a long silence, the alpha replied to Charlie with a few gentle yips of friendship and then with his family gathered about him he calmly led them away. Soon all had disappeared into an area of rough ice to the north. We had, by chance, stumbled onto a spot that we judged to be a resting area for the wolf family. The alpha led his family across the frozen ocean. They had cleverly discovered easier hunting via following the bears and shared food whenever the opportunity arose. Apparently sensing that he had been accepted by the alpha leader, with a tug on his leash Charlie urged us to follow. "No, Charlie, not this time," I said quietly. Clearly disappointed, Charlie continued at my side, but with frequent glances in the direction the wolves had taken.

Later we approached Richards Island in a shadowless ice fog that slowed our progress to a blind crawl. We could scarcely see our outstretched hands. Depth perception had disappeared. Up and down, east, west, north and south were all the same. White walls of dense ice crystals closed in from all directions. We drifted in a silent void. I stopped and shook my head to rid myself of a wave of vertigo.

"I hardly know whether I'm standing up straight," Bill said as he groped his way forward. "I feel as if I'm floating." Even the ice underfoot was obscured.

Each step was an adventure, like walking on a cloud. We nervously worried about polar bears that could approach unseen. More than ever, we would have to rely on Charlie to warn us. Seven nerve-wrecking hours later our GPS unit said that we had passed Richards Island, which lay hidden behind the wall of white to our left. Now our boots crunched across the thin coastal ice of Pullen Island. We retreated to more stable ice to set up camp just as dusk darkened our claustrophobic world. There was no wind and for once the ice was still. We hoped that improved visibility would arrive by morning so that we could see the nearby island.

Although troubled by the fog and the fear of bears, we rested well for the first two hours. But then Charlie rose and listened at the door. His head turned to the right and then to the left as if following something unseen outside. We reached for our shotguns and waited silently, wondering if it was a bear or a wolf. After five or ten minutes that seemed to last forever Charlie relaxed. His tail fanned back and forth, and after two soft yips he returned to my sleeping bag and with a contented sigh resumed his sleep. Now we were convinced that wolves had paid us a visit and Charlie had recognized them as friendly. Sleep came only fitfully for the rest of the night. Dawn greeted us with the same silent dense mist. After a short discussion, and although disappointed at not seeing the two islands, we decided to begin our journey back the mainland. As I loaded my sleeping bag onto my sled, I looked down. Right beside the runners was a large set of polar bear prints and two sets of wolf tracks that continued right past our tent only three feet in front of the door. Now the nighttime picture was clear. Charlie must have known there was a bear outside, but had sensed that it presented no danger and had greeted the two wolves following behind.

The presence of bears and the persistent heavy fog made us suspect that there was a large expanse of open water nearby, possibly to the north. Perhaps last night's visitors were passing through on their way to another seal hunting area. Charlie showed no signs of scenting bears but we decided to head south as quickly as possible.

We fumbled our way along. Charlie suddenly stopped, his tail gently wagging back and forth. He yipped twice and was answered by several wolf voices close by to our right. Then, with his head proudly erect, Charlie stepped in front to lead us, as if to display his alpha status. We suspected that these wolves already knew us and were no threat to us. They might have been following us out of natural curiosity. If so, Charlie seemed happy to have them close by. The possibility that they were following a bear also occurred to us. All we could do about the latter was to rely on Charlie's highly tuned senses to warn us if we encountered danger. His relaxed attitude and occasional friendly tail wagging gestures over the next hour convinced us that we were being accompanied by wolves and not bears. All that day we struggled through dense fog and across ice that showed frequent splits and gaps that forced us to make detours. We decided to camp rather than risk mishap in the uncertain conditions.

Halfway through dinner, the distant rumble of breaking ice grew louder. The fog muffled the sound but it seemed to be coming from the west. In case another major ice breakup was on its way we raced to break camp, load the sleds, and set a course to the east, adrenaline speeding us away—we hoped to safety. Bill led, while I skied practically on his heels with Charlie at my side. All around us the ice quivered and moved. Suddenly we were in the midst of an ice eruption. Ready to run if needed, we ripped off our skis and lashed them to our sleds. Then a ghostly moan came from the direction of a pressure ridge we had just crossed. As we watched in disbelief the whole thing collapsed on itself with a thunderous roar, sending blinding particles of snow and ice dust into our faces. Charlie pressed close to my side, afraid. A hundred feet away, a flat area suddenly erupted upward under powerful pressure from the ocean depths. Plates of ice rose and slammed on top of each other. We hurdled a wide crack. In front of us a ridge jerked fifty feet apart. Bill yelled, "Run!" Racing for an opening in the ridges with Charlie in the lead we escaped across an ice bridge just before tons of ice slammed behind us. We leaped over a three-foot chasm dunking the tails of our sleds into the dark water as we barely jerked them across to solid ice. Still the ice moved about us. Charlie close at my side, we followed Bill as he searched for an escape route to dodge the violent eruptions and widening cracks. After what seemed an eternity, the sounds of erupting ice slowly faded into the distance. Physically and emotionally drained, we collapsed onto our sleds thankful to be alive.

The fog was being driven away by a new stiff breeze. With vastly improved visibility we searched for a safe camp site, but in the chaos there was none. We pressed on, looking for routes through ridges and pinnacles of ice carved into an endless array of abstract shapes and sizes. An hour later, nearing exhaustion, we still struggled to heave our sleds up and over yet another ridge and through more teetering ice blocks. Even Charlie was tired. Darkness had descended, leaving only the reflection from the ice to give us a little gray light. By now the stiff breeze had become a strong wind that blasted our bodies with waves of spindrift. A layer of ice shrouded Charlie's thick coat; his face was a white mask. The fog had completely disappeared in the gale. Cresting another pressure ridge, we headed for a level area ahead. Although a sloping ice pan, it was the best we had seen in a long time.

Putting the tent up was an adventure and a test of persistence, to say the least. The howling wind tore at the tent, trying to rip it from our grasp. Bill threw his body across the fabric to hold it down while I grabbed the ice screws and fixed them into the ice. The tent was barely erect when Charlie pushed his way through the partly open doorway. He was tired and obviously wanted to be finished with the day. After a few bites of his food he was asleep on my sleeping bag even before Bill and I had finished the last crumbs of our day's ration of food bars. Finally we climbed into our sleeping bags. My attempt to shove Charlie over and claim my full share of our bed was a complete failure. He merely spread out and, fast asleep, lay his head on me. I gave up and slid into the narrow sliver he had left for me.

Next morning, we were rewarded with an expanded world of blue skies and visibility that stretched to the horizon. Ahead, along our route south, only a half mile away, was an immense area of open water. Closing in on the chasm, it showed itself to be more than a mile long and at least a half mile wide. Six polar bears paced along the edges hunting seals as a close watch was kept by arctic foxes and the wolves we recognized as members if the ice pack family.

Charlie stopped to watch, then raised his muzzle to catch any incoming scents. After sending a few yips of greeting to the wolves, he walked on without so much as another glance in their direction. The wolves looked up as we approached. The alpha took a couple of steps toward us and returned Charlie's yips as if greeting a friend. Charlie showed no concern over the bears, so we too walked on—glad to be leaving the area. We continued to marvel at Charlie's ability to find acceptance among wild wolves. When we had first decided to bring Charlie with us on our year-long wolf study we knew that he might not be accepted and could have been in serious danger. It was an experiment that had evolved and succeeded beyond our wildest dreams. Now he had been accepted by a second wolf pack.

Our southern route back to the Mackenzie Delta took us over the best ice we had so far encountered on the entire expedition. We looked forward to meeting John and to establishing Wolf Camp Two close to the delta wolf pack he had been studying for several years.

Charlie shows two sides of his character

Camp Two — McKenzie comes close to investigate

Chapter Twenty —
Wolf Camp Two

Later, after a long and uneventful ski journey back to the mainland, we pitched our tent in a place John had marked on our maps and where he would meet us in a few days.

Just as he had at Wolf Camp One, Charlie carefully marked his boundary all around our tent area. After inspecting the entire site, he scent-marked our tent on three sides. "Oh boy, here we go again," Bill said. With his territory adequately claimed, Charlie sat expectantly outside the tent door, appearing to wait for the appearance of visitors he seemed certain were close among the nearby trees. After an hour we glimpsed a lone wolf gliding through the deep shadows of the forest.

At midnight, the sky was transformed with a tapestry of dazzling northern lights. Charlie stepped outside the tent and stared intently at the area to our right. We followed his gaze and detected a slight movement. Charlie howled. Minutes later came a single call, then quiet yips from a second wolf. After a few minutes of quiet, Charlie returned inside, and we followed. But sleep didn't come easily when we knew that wolves were watching us from amid the nearby trees.

Next morning in the early light, a sudden chorus erupted. Six wolves stood at the edge of the forest, howling. The moment we stepped out of the tent, they stopped abruptly and exchanged stares with Charlie. Within seconds Charlie sat down and turned his head to the side to avoid direct eye contact. We settled on our sleds and we too looked away submissively. Two wolves stepped a little closer but froze in place when we looked directly at them. Then the six quietly spread out, but remained close to the security of the woods. They moved without aggression, but with nervous curiosity. After a few minutes Charlie rose, tail curled high above his back to signal his alpha status. He immediately became the sole focus of attention. A male, mostly blond with gray markings and clearly their alpha, approached alone—stiff-legged and cautious—to sniff and then re-sniff Charlie's laid-out scent marks, and then re-mark some with his own scent. Then he returned to his family, who had watched from the trees. Charlie, with a hint of arrogance, turned his back and strolled into the tent. He reappeared a few minutes later, still under the scrutiny of the wolves, none of whom had taken their eyes off the tent when Charlie disappeared into it. The dominant male again faced Charlie, but now slowly waved his tail. The two appeared to have accepted each other. We were thrilled and surprised that positive contact with the alpha had occurred so soon. To signify the end of the visit, Charlie re-entered the tent and lay down on his customary place on my sleeping bag. The alpha, finding himself ignored, led his pack into the woods.

Now that we had established successful contact, we re-read the notes John had written about his experiences and what we might expect from this delta pack. Over the next few days Bill and I were careful to move slowly around our tent area. Charlie spent much of his time quietly watching wolves come and go. The alpha male, a magnificent animal with a thick, blond neck ruff, we named Mackenzie after the river that coursed through the delta that he and his family called home. He was a laid-back leader and appeared to have accepted Charlie as an alpha. He became the center of Charlie's attention. It was clear that they had established some sort of bond.

Mackenzie was the only one to approach Charlie's scent marks surrounding our tent area during the next several days. He gave Bill and me only sporadic glances of appraisal. He and his family were used to seeing John and apparently judged that we also presented no threat. He concentrated his gaze on Charlie, who seemed to fascinate him. The rest of the family were cautious for the first week, but they quickly followed their leader's easy approach and soon settled down to a routine of watching us from the edge of the forest that was their home between hunts.

As with the summer pack, they were a playful lot and often teased each other into an energetic game of chase. It was entertaining and often comical to watch their human-like play. One would hide behind a tree and leap out at an unsuspecting victim. After rolling and wrestling in the snow, suddenly the game stopped and the participants shook themselves free of snow and then awaited further victims.

The day arrived for John to join us. He pitched his tent alongside ours. We were eager to share with him the details of our experience watching bears and wolves and the seal hunts. John was fascinated to learn of Charlie's acceptance by the ice wolf pack, and now he quickly saw that Charlie had been accepted by the delta pack, especially Mackenzie.

It wasn't long before Mackenzie showed signs of trying to convince Charlie to join him. While John watched the two, he told us, "This fellow used to be a beta animal and was never a leader. He only took over as leader after the last one was killed in a fight with a stranger from another pack. Now I can see that he recognizes Charlie as a strong-willed alpha and seems to be inviting him to take over. Never in all my years around wolves have I ever seen anything so remarkable." More than ever, John understood how Charlie had paved the way for our success.

Just as he had during the summer, John sat outside his tent and sang soft Inuit songs. It was clear that these wolves knew him just as the summer wolves had. Their heads went up, their ears pointed forward, and they appeared to relax as they listened to the quiet singing. Then, quite casually, this man of few words simply said, "They calm down when I sing." It didn't surprise us when one day John told us, "I'm more comfortable around wolves than I am around humans."

One night while we wrote in our journals in the dim light of a tiny candle that threatened to go out at any moment, we noticed a laser-like beam of light penetrating the tent walls. In a minute we were outside, gasping at the sight above us. The northern lights, or aurora borealis, sent an immense curtain of soft green light pulsating across the sky, wavering in delicate curves as if it were a bridal train filling the heavens, swirling and moving to a silent script. A soft rose color gradually washed across the green, only to retreat a little, as if to share the universe with the green that now pulsated in unison with the rose. Although the lower edge of these auroral displays usually don't reach closer than a hundred miles above the surface of the earth, the bottom of this one seemed to brush the horizon; at the top, the lights curved out to the infinity of space. The northern lights are created by charged particles that penetrate the atmosphere along the magnetic fields of the polar regions, creating a solar wind circling the earth at high latitudes. The enormous wall of light, sometimes several hundred miles long and at times more than 150 miles high, moves in waves across the heavens. Mesmerized, we ignored the chill of the night air. The pulsating curtain drifted away as if to leave us, only to return, all the while moving back and forth in great folds and curves. Eventually, as the light faded to a dark sky full of stars, we returned to our sleeping bags, cold but in awe. Of all the auroras we had seen, this was perhaps the most spectacular.

Two days later in the breaking dawn, we heard a frenzy of excited howling. The entire pack was gathering to leave on a hunt. We had been waiting for this moment! Grabbing backpacks that we had already prepared for a quick exit, we set out following John, who took Charlie's lead to follow a narrow trail that led away from our campsite across the flat tundra and over a low willow-covered rise. The wolves traveled single file, stepping in the same snow tracks to conserve energy. Only the front wolf broke trail, and when he tired, another would take his place. Their wide paws helped them stay close to the surface of the soft snow. Cutting across a frozen lake we reached a low sedge-covered hill from where, with the aid of binoculars, we watched the pack set out in determined pursuit of a lone moose. But the animal sped away and quickly outdistanced the wolves. Undaunted, the wolves streaked across the frozen tundra to intercept another moose that had broken away from a small group. To escape the enemy, the animal veered away, but soon floundered in a trough of deep snow. Before it could reach firmer ground, the pursuing wolves caught up to the fleeing animal, which quickly went down under a mass of six wolves, while the rest of the herd dashed away to safety. The wolves' speed, even in winter conditions, was impressive. Intent on joining the feasting wolves, an excited Charlie pulled John toward them, almost causing him to stumble as Charlie leaped to the end of his lead. Quickly recovering, John pulled back, with the three of us shouting, "No, Charlie!" Completely deaf to our commands, Charlie continued to bark in protest and strain ahead. I stepped forward and grabbed his lead, but he ignored my demand that he turn back.

While my voice rose in indignation, Charlie grudgingly turned away with an attitude of sullen discontent and agreed to follow me, but with no air of forgiveness. John was mesmerized. "I've never seen anything like it. He's totally in step with these wolves. Out here I bet he even thinks like a wolf, or maybe he thinks he is a wolf." Leaving the wolves to enjoy their feast, we headed back to camp with Charlie reluctantly following at my heels. The snowstorm, which had been only an occasional snowflake as we left camp, had now increased as the wind whistled across the open tundra. The sharp bite of wind-driven snow in our faces made us hurry to the shelter of our tents.

Halfway back, a snowy owl settled down amid a clump of sedge, as silent as a puff of thistledown. This new and fascinating opportunity to chase a bird, a species that he usually regarded with disdain, electrified Charlie into instant action. His leap forward was so unexpected that his lead tore from my hand as he made a fervent sprint after the startled bird. With a loud squawk the bird rose and banked sharply away just as Charlie, with a loud snap of his jaws, barely missed. Although unsuccessful in his quest, the incident served to change his disposition from one of grudging obedience to one of magnanimous victory at having sent a creature that sat low on his social scale to flee in haste. With Charlie in the lead, tail held high, apparently having forgiven his human companions' transgressions, we reached our campsite in time to escape the full strength of the storm, which built to a shrieking crescendo of wind and snow and kept us tent-bound for three days.

Two weeks later, on a moonlit 19-degree night in mid-March, the sound of thundering hooves awoke us. We leaped to the door as the tent was bumped by an unseen body. Grabbing the shotgun, Bill was first out the door followed by

Charlie and me. Caribou swept past both sides of the tent with the wolves right on their heels. The frenzied caribou reached the forest at full speed and fled into the night. The hunters closed on the straggler. The sounds of leaping wolves and the desperate cries of an animal going down cleaved the still air. The wolves gorged themselves.

Charlie, caught up in the excitement, tugged hard at his leash. We pulled on our boots and allowed him to lead us closer to the feasting wolves, stopping a few yards away. Mackenzie looked up, saw that it was Charlie, and turned his attention back to gulping down the meat. Returning to the tent with a reluctant Charlie following, we discovered two bent pegs where the caribou had hit the tent. After Bill straightened them, we resumed our sleep. The next morning Charlie discovered a gift. A portion of the caribou's hind leg lay at his boundary. Mackenzie watched from the edge of the trees as Charlie picked it up, then lay alongside the tent to enjoy his gift of fresh meat. Once, when Charlie paused to look across to him, Mackenzie gently fanned his tail. It was a moment of unwavering friendship between the two.

By the end of March, the deep chill of midwinter had passed, and our rations were stretched to the limit. With approach of the spring thaw we needed to leave while the snow and ice were stable enough to safely cross small streams and areas of boggy marsh. John left on his snowmobile for Inuvik, where we would meet him again on our way home. It was time for us to leave Charlie's new friends. They appeared to sense that we were leaving and all watched from the edge of the trees. Charlie quietly returned their stare. While we loaded our gear onto our sleds, of course Charlie too knew we were leaving. Mackenzie paced back and forth and quietly yipped. Charlie fanned his tail in answer.

We finished securing our loads and clipped on our skis. As we had with the summer pack, we said goodbye to each individual and promised to return with John the next winter. It was so hard to leave. Charlie stopped several times to look back, as if wanting one last look at his friends. Willow, Mackenzie's mate, stood at the edge of the clearing with the family, and Mackenzie followed a hundred feet behind our sleds. We climbed a low rise and descended the other side. Mackenzie stood motionless, tall and regal on the crest against the backdrop of blue sky. After several minutes he turned back to his family. It broke our hearts to see him leave. Bill led and we skied single-file, too sad to talk. Charlie walked quietly at my side without looking back. I could feel his sadness, but he seemed to have accepted that we were going home.

An hour later, we were surprised to suddenly see the wolves flitting noiselessly through the trees to our left. Mackenzie had returned with his entire family to say one last goodbye. Charlie stopped, sat on his haunches, and raised his muzzle in one last sorrowful howl to his friends, who answered in a long wailing chorus. With tears, we bade our friends farewell again. Then Willow touched her shoulder gently to her mate's. Mackenzie, who had blossomed into a gentle if reluctant leader, turned and led his family away with Willow at his side. She seemed to know that Mackenzie longed for Charlie to stay, and comforted him with little brushes to his muzzle. It was a heart-wrenching display of true devotion.

It had been a happy year for Charlie. It was clear that his distant wolf genes gave him an understanding and a place in the life of wolves. Charlie, with his wolf heritage and his intelligent gentle nature, had allowed our dream to become a reality.

After we returned home, Charlie resumed his role as alpha among the dogs and continued to hike many miles to lakes and mountains in the Cascade Mountains. In addition to accompanying me to schools where I presented lectures, he visited nursing homes, children's hospitals, and camps for special needs children. He was the star of numerous fundraising events. When I was a keynote speaker at many corporate conventions Charlie always received a special invitation. He had an aura about him that made people want to kneel and hug him. He even received cards from his fans all over the world. He wasn't just a dog: to many he was a true hero, just as he was to Bill and me. He never did accept the back seat of the car. He was our pilot, and only the front seat would do!

After much discussion, Bill and I decided the story of our time with the wolf packs would be best told in a full-length book devoted to our year-long adventure, and we would name the book Three Among the Wolves. Once more Charlie was the star, just as he was in my first book, Polar Dream.

Charlie celebrated his twenty-third birthday in 2003. He always enjoyed excellent health, perhaps due to abundant exercise, home-cooked food, and his monthly visits to his acupuncturist and chiropractor. We had returned home from a hike to one of his favorite mountain lakes, and that evening after he had finished his dinner he went to his usual place in our bedroom and fell fast asleep—a peaceful ending to an amazing life of adventure and love.

His passing left a huge void in our lives. He had played a vital part in our daily activities, so much so that at first I could not imagine a life without him. He had been a major part of my life for so long, but as the pain of his passing eased, we realized what a privilege it had been for us to share many amazing and happy years with him. Spiritually he has never left us. He lies at peace in a special place in a peaceful grove on our farm, overlooking the mountains he loved. He will always walk at our sides in spirit. His uncanny intelligence, along with his unfailing devotion to Bill and me, will continue to guide our path until we all meet again.

He will always be the hero by my side.

Epilogue

Reflections

Over many years of worldwide expeditions, I have had the opportunity to reflect on the many times I have stepped out of my comfort zone. Although I am proud of the fact that I was the first woman to solo any of the world's poles when I skied with Charlie to the magnetic North Pole, the reason for my journey and the effect it has had on my life since then goes far beyond being "first." Accomplishing a "first" was not the most important outcome, but rather the experience of the journey and the valuable lessons I learned.

To this day I am grateful for the close bond that developed so quickly between Charlie and me. This amazing dog had a profound impact on my life as much as the expedition itself. As we traveled day after day to the Pole, I learned that humans have a lot to learn from our canine friends; unconditional trust, love and a friendship that never ceases.

The lessons I learned in a mid-winter climb of Mount Taranaki in New Zealand at age nine still ring true. Half way to the summit my young legs had turned leaden with fatigue. My father kept telling me, "It takes only one step at a time to reach the top." My mother urged me to visualize myself standing on the summit, "Keep a picture of it in your mind as you climb." Those two lessons took me to the summit and became an important contribution to my later success in major worldwide expeditions.

As an adult, an international athlete and mountain climber, I learned, that although setting goals is important to our progress through life, a goal without a well thought out plan is only a dream. And once setting out, never look back at failures and difficulties. Always look forward to success.

The journey to the Pole gave me a new awareness and greater confidence to push the limits of challenge. To reach the Pole I had to face the extreme challenge of fear as Charlie and I were confronted by polar bears. I soon discovered that it's okay to be afraid. It's how we handle our fear that will determine our success.

Now I am an eighty-three-year-old adventurer still a work in progress. I continue to set goals and travel paths that take me to remote places. I still have many hundreds of miles to walk as I continue to develop educational programs for Adventure Classroom, a program I began in 1988. I can easily relate to those in middle age and beyond who question their goals and dreams. Through experience I am convinced that age is no barrier to our dreams and goals.

About the Author

New Zealand born Helen Thayer's life is a testament to setting goals and achieving them. She climbed her first mountain at nine years old. A family friend, Sir Edmund Hillary, became her mentor and teacher of mountain climbing skills.

As an athlete, Thayer represented three countries in international track and field. After moving to the United States, she won the U.S. National Luge Championship in 1975 and was a member of the national team. Later in 1990, Helen was the American team leader of the first women's Russian-American Arctic Expedition.

She has received many awards and accolades including National Geographic/National Public Radio naming Helen as "One of the great explorers of the 20th Century."

The "Outstanding Achievement Award" by the American Mountain Foundation, now the Rocky Mountain Field Institute.

Honored at a White House reception by President Clinton as "A Woman who Dared."

The "Vancouver Award" by the Explorers Club for "An explorer who has contributed to the pursuit of knowledge and demonstrated the spirit of exploration."

The Alaskan Geographic Alliance "The Robert Henning Award" for "Education and Exploration."

Wings World Quest "Lifetime Award" "For a lifetime of Exploration and Education."

With presentations to audiences worldwide, she has addressed countless organizations of all ages from one-room schools in the Amazon to the Kremlin and White House.

At age fifty she began her world-wide expedition career. A partial list of her historical expeditions includes:

First woman to travel alone to any of the world's Poles when she skied at age fifty to the magnetic North Pole without dog sled, snowmobile, resupply or support.

First woman to walk 4,000 miles across the Sahara from Morocco to the Nile River.

At age sixty-three the first woman to walk 1,600 miles across the Gobi Desert.

Kayaked 2,200 miles of the Amazon River at age seventy.

In a unique study of wolves, Helen lived among wolves above the Arctic Circle for a year in a quest to study wolves in the wild.

At age eighty, in 2017, Helen became the first person to walk solo the full length of Death Valley. She repeated the journey in 2018, with her companion dog Sam. These two treks were the first in a continuing American National Park series of educational programs and videos.

Helen can be reached at www.helenthayer.com.

Helen's books have been translated into ten languages and include:

Polar Dream, Three Among the Wolves, Walking the Gobi.

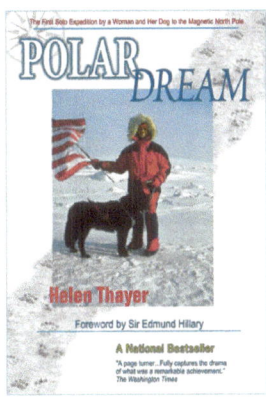
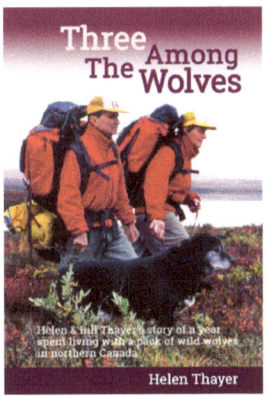
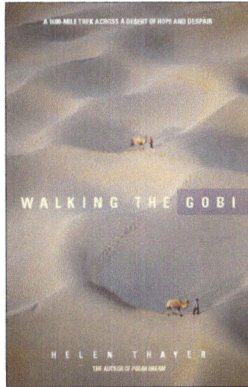

The Photographs in the Arctic

To document my solo expedition I carried a lightweight tripod with a remote control unit which I carefully situated on level ice for self-portraits. For the hand-held shots I used a Nikon FM2 camera body, which was the workhorse of cold weather photography. It works even when the batteries are cold and dead. My lenses included a wide-angle, 20-mm lens, a 28 to 210 mm lens, and a 300 mm lens for telephoto shots, along with a polarizer filter.

While underway, the camera sat cushioned in my sleeping bag on top of my sled, where I could quickly unzip the cover and take a photograph within a few seconds. I returned home with a photographic account of my journey which I have shared in lectures world-wide to audiences of all ages.

www.ingramcontent.com/pod-product-compliance
Lightning Source LLC
Chambersburg PA
CBHW050738110526
44590CB00002B/19